Yasodharā,

the Wife of the Bōdhisattva

Yasodharā, the Wife of the Bōdhisattva

THE SINHALA *Yasodharāvata*
(The Story of Yasodharā)
AND THE SINHALA *Yasodharāpadānaya*
(The Sacred Biography of Yasodharā)

Translated with an Introduction and Notes by
RANJINI OBEYESEKERE

STATE UNIVERSITY OF NEW YORK PRESS

COVER ART: The Buddha visits his former wife and son, approximately 100-300. Pakistan; former kingdom of Gandhara. Frieze; phyllite. The Avery Brundage Collection, B60S283. © Asian Art Museum of San Francisco. Used by permission.

Published by
STATE UNIVERSITY OF NEW YORK PRESS, ALBANY

Printed in the United States of America

For information, contact State University of New York Press, Albany, NY
www.sunypress.edu

Production and book design, Laurie Searl
Marketing, Michael Campochiaro

Library of Congress Cataloging in Publication Data

Yasodharāvata. English.

Yasodharā, the wife of the Bōdhisattva : the Sinhala Yasodharāvata (the story of Yasodharā) and the Sinhala Yasodharāpadānaya (the sacred biography of Yasodharā) / Ranjini Obeyesekere.

p. cm.

Includes bibliographical references.

ISBN 978-1-4384-2827-7 (hardcover : alk. paper)

ISBN 978-1-4384-2828-4 (pbk. : alk. paper) 1. Sinhalese literature—Translations into English. I. Obeyesekere, Ranjini. II. Yasodharapadanaya. English. III. Title.

PK2859.Y38E5 2009

891.4'808—dc22

2009000585

10 9 8 7 6 5 4 3 2 1

To my sisters Damayanthi Ratwatte and Savitri Goonesekere

with much affection and admiration for their outstanding contributions

each to their own world.

Contents

Preface

This manuscript has undergone several incarnations. Many years ago I translated a few verses popularly known in the folk repertoire as the *Yasodharā vilāpaya* or Yasodharā's lament. They were verses that had always moved me and so I translated them into English as part of a collection of folk poems I had worked on from time to time when the mood took me.

Then about twenty years later a friend who had seen my earlier translation suggested that I translate the full *Yasodharāvata* poem. I agreed and began work on a translation of what I then realized was a long narrative poem. It took some years to do as I found several sections of the poem fairly pedestrian and lost interest, unlike with the verses of the lament that had so moved me. I tried to keep that translation as close to the original as possible as I wanted it to be published side by side with the Sinhala text. It was published in Sri Lanka in 2005 together with the Sinhala text. The present translation is less rigidly tied to the text, though I hope not a less accurate rendering of the poem's meaning and emotional content.

While working on the translation, I was struck by what I felt were a series of additions or layering that seemed to have taken place over time. This led me to explore early manuscript versions of the poem in the National Museum Library in Colombo and the British Museum Library in London. It was then that I came across several manuscripts listed under the title *Yasodharāvata* but dealing with a different text, the *Yasodharāpadāna*. One section, which had seemed to me as I worked on the poem to be a later addition, struck me then as based on material found in the *Yasodharāpadāna*, incidents and events in Yasodharā's life as a nun that were not very familiar at the folk level. I felt this section could have been an addition to the folk poem by a monk transcriber familiar with the *Yasodhrāpadānaya* text. I decided therefore to translate the Sinhala *Yasodharāpadānaya* both out of interest for its content and to illustrate this connection with the *Yasodharāvata* poem.

Doing some further research for an introduction to the two texts I had translated, I became fascinated with how the shadowy figure of Yasodharā, wife of the Bōdhisattva, of whom there is scarce mention in the very earliest strata of the Buddhist canon, does enter the body of canonical Buddhist literature from around the first century CE. She is first introduced in her role as a nun and an *arahat,* an aspect of her character that could legitimately be expanded on by early Buddhist monks. Then, like monks and laymen for generations after, fascinated by this woman of great devotion and powerful character, I too began to follow the different accounts of her in a series of texts—the first or second century Pali *Yasodharāpadāna*, the cameo portrait in the Sanskrit poet Ashvaghosa's *Buddhacarita*, the *Mahāvagga* account of her refusal to go hear the Buddha preach on his return after the Enlightenment, the Sinhala *Yasodharāpadānaya*, which is an expansion of the Pali text of the same name, the chapter in the thirteenth century Sinhala *Pūjāvaliya* that expands on her character, the accounts in the Sanskrit *Bhadrakalpāvadāna*, and the *Sanghabēdavastu* section of the *Mūlasarvastivāda* texts, and finally the seventeenth, eighteenth, or nineteenth century folk poems from Thailand and Sri Lanka. It is no doubt an eclectic collection of texts encountered in my work on the *Yasodharāvata*, but they do provide an account of the continuing fascination that both monks and laypersons had for this woman of extraordinary devotion and moral courage.

I include extracts from these texts in my introduction in order to show the figure of Yasodharā as she appears first in the early Buddhist literature. I then trace her story as it occurs in early Sinhala literature, extracts of which I have translated. The folk poem *Yasodharāvata* can thus be seen in the larger context of the Buddhist and Sinhala literary traditions. I also discuss the possible incorporation or extraction of a section of this folk poem into the tradition of funeral laments or *vilāpa*, as these verses are still sung or chanted at village funerals. I then give a detailed analysis of the poem as it exists today.

Chapter 1 is a translation of the folk poem *Yasodharāvata.* This translation is less rigidly tied to the original text than my earlier version, though I hope no less accurate. I have brief footnotes of explanation that might help a general non-specialist reader who may not have the background to access and appreciate the poem. Chapter 2 has a brief comment on the Sinhala *Yasodharāpadānaya*, followed in chapter 3 by a translation of the thirteenth century Sinhala text. I decided to translate the Sinhala *Yasodharāpadānaya* text in full because it is a *version*, not just a translation, of the Pali *Yasodharāpadāna* and hence provides interesting comparative material.

In an appendix I present a detailed discussion of the palm leaf manuscripts entitled *Yasodharāvata* that I found in the National Museum Library in Sri Lanka and at the British Museum Library in London. The material may not be of interest to the general reader, but may have some use for scholars.

Finally I have a glossary of Buddhist terms and concepts that are referred to in my translation of the texts.

As noted earlier, this work started as a simple translation of a section of a poem. As my interest in the figure of Yasodharā grew and the research around it expanded, the final manuscript has become a more extended account of the woman Yasodharā and her growing presence in the literature and the imagination of later generations.

Translations are never an adequate transference of the original literary work. All translators accept this impossibility as a given. But they are the only means one has to access the literatures of other cultures whose languages one does not know and is unlikely to learn. We translators continue to grapple with the endlessly challenging activity of trying to achieve the best possible approximation of an original work of literature that has moved us, hoping to make it accessible to a wider readership. This is my only justification for having attempted these translations and I hope that readers will capture something of what the original was like, as a result of, or in spite of, my translation.

RANJINI OBEYESEKERE
KANDY, SRI LANKA

Acknowledgments

An earlier version of parts of the introduction and some of the verses of my translation of the *Yasodharāvata* have appeared in two other publications: in the appendix to my book *Modern Sinhala Writing and the New Critics* (Colombo: Gunasena, 1974) and in *Yasodharāvata (The Story of Yasodharā or Yasodharā's Lament*) (Colombo: Godage, 2005).

I would like to remember here the late Bandula Jayawardene who first urged me to translate the poem *Yasodharāvata.*

I wish to thank especially my longtime friend and colleague Professor Ratna Handurukande. We have worked together on translations since the days when we were young lecturers at the University of Peradeniya, where we would sit in the shade of a tree on that lovely campus, share a lunch, and work on a text. My translation of the *Yasodharāpadānaya* owes much to her rigorous scholarship and careful reading of my manuscript.

I would also like to thank Professor Piyaseeli Wijemane for her comments and insights; Professor Tissa Kumara for his help with the Pali stanzas in the *apadāna* text; Professor Patrick Olivelle for generously allowing me to use sections of his then-unpublished translation of the *Buddhacarita*; Dr. J. Tattleman and Dr. Sally Mellick Cutler for giving me access to their work on Yasodharā (published and unpublished); Profesor Charles Hallisey and Professor Don Swearer for reading and commenting on the introduction to my text; and Dr. Lakshmi de Silva for her continuing support and encouragement of my work of translation.

Professor Hildred Geertz and Dr. Priscilla Barnum, my friends and colleagues in Princeton, spent many hours going through initial versions of the translation with me, pointing out where a general reader unfamiliar with Buddhist concepts would have problems understanding my translation. Their insights highlighted much that I took for granted and so had failed to see.

Thanks are also due to Aparna Silva Kishore for her help with locating the palm leaf manuscripts at the National Museum Library; Sonali Deraniyagala, Carol Zanca, and Mo lin Yi, for assistance with the final chores of formatting the manuscript for publication; and Nancy Ellegate and the publishing team at SUNY Press for the readiness with which they have accepted my translations of Buddhist literary works from the Sinhala.

Finally, to Gananath, for being there for me.

Introduction

YASODHARĀ: THE WOMAN

Many Sri Lankans of my generation, who grew up hearing folk songs sung to them as lullabies or learned them in school in later childhood, will remember verses from the *Yasodharāvata*. We knew only a few verses, excerpts that had entered the folk repertoire, but the melancholy rhythms of Yasodharā's lament haunted my childhood imagination and left a lasting resonance.

Yasodharā is the name in Buddhist literature for the wife of Prince Siddharta, the Bōdhisattva[1] who later became the Buddha Gautama. Although there is virtually no reference to Yasodharā in the earliest texts of the Pali canon, in the Buddha narrative, as it has come down in the canonical tradition, Yasodharā does appear, first only as the nun Rāhula mātā (mother of Rāhula) and later as Yasodharā or Bimbā, the wife of the Bōdhisattva.

The Buddha narrative's central focus is necessarily on the Bōdhisattva Siddharta. It is his extraordinary birth, his life as a royal prince, his renunciation of the luxuries of that life, his renunciation even of his wife and son whom he loves dearly that are extolled. The story describes also the many years spent in futile and extreme asceticism, his achievement of Buddhahood, his subsequent life as a teacher, and final death. His wife, Yasodharā, appears only as a shadowy figure in that larger, more important, story.

1. The *Bōdhisattva*, also termed the *Bōsat* in Sinhala, is one who strives through many lives in *saṃsāra* to cultivate the perfect virtues necessary to become a Buddha.

There is one scene in the life of the Bōdhisattva Siddharta—that of the "great renunciation" (*mahābhinikmaṇa*)—that appears again and again in literature and art throughout the Buddhist world. It is the scene where the Bōdhisattva goes to bid farewell to his wife and newborn son. Even there, the beautiful Yasodharā is a non-actor. She is asleep. We see her only through his eyes—the young and lovely wife he must leave if he is to keep his resolve to become a Buddha.

Thereafter the figure of Yasodharā disappears from the official Buddha story only to make one last fleeting appearance as part of the entourage of women who go to the Buddha seeking permission to be ordained as Buddhist nuns. There too she is a minor figure, unlike Prajāpati Gōtami, the Buddha's foster mother, who becomes head of the order. All we are told is that Yasodharā becomes a nun and later an *arahat* (an Enlightened One).

The woman Yasodharā may occupy only a small space in the early Buddha narrative, but her elusive figure has continued to fascinate Buddhists over the centuries. The many retellings of her story in prose and verse, by both monks and laymen throughout the Buddhist world, are evidence of this fascination. These accounts focus on certain critical lacunae in her story, given passing mention in the larger narrative but that provide possibilities for expansion by later monastic and lay commentators.

YAṢODHARĀ IN EARLY SANSKRIT AND PALI BUDDHIST LITERATURE

a) The Pali Yasodharāpadāna

As the canonical literature develops over time, Yasodharā's figure takes on a life and a persona. One of the earliest of such extensions concerns her life as a nun. In the Pali *Yasodharāpadāna*[2] (sacred biography of Yasodharā) dated around the first century CE and found among the apadāna texts in the *Khuddaka Nikāya* that deal with the lives of the Elders (monks and nuns) of the Pali Theravada tradition, there is an account of Yasodharā the *arahat*. There we are told that, on the day she is to die, the nun Yasodharā goes to make her final farewell to the Buddha, displays her supernormal magical powers before a gathered assembly of monks, nuns, and laypersons, and then goes on to recount her many acts of devotion to the Bōdhisattva in their journey through *saṃsāra*.

---

2. The *Apadāna* of the *Khuddaka Nikāya* edited by M. E. Lilley. London: Pali Text Society, 1925.

There are many versions of the *Yasodharāpadāna* in prose and verse and in several languages. This early Pali collection seems to have provided a space, especially for monks, to imaginatively expand upon her life. The attribution of miraculous powers gives her a further dimension. No longer is she the shadowy figure of the early Buddhist texts. The Apadana transforms her into an exceptional and powerful almost divine being.

b) Ashvaghosa's Buddhacarita

Another very early commentary that introduces the figure of Yasodharā, not as a nun but as the grieving wife in the Buddha story, is the Sanskrit poem titled *Buddhacarita* (life of the Buddha) by the Mahayāna monk Ashvaghosa dated between the first and second century CE. In it there is a section titled "Lamenting in the Seraglio"[3] in which the women of the palace, Prajāpati Gōtami, his foster mother, and Yasodharā, his chief queen, lament the Bōdhisattva's departure in his quest for Enlightenment. The theme of Yasodharā's grief and her lament at the departure of her husband is yet another point of possible expansion that captured the imagination of poets very early in their recounting of the Buddha narrative. One is struck by the way in which not just the events of the Bōdhisattva's life but certain themes in the women's laments filter down through these early texts, tenuous threads that surface again and again in much later works in far-flung areas of the Buddhist world.

One such example is Yasodharā's initial anger at the minister Chandaka (s: Canna, pronounced Channa) who returns without the Bōdhisattva. The poet of the *Buddhacarita* has Yasodharā make him the scapegoat for the departure of her lord.

Canto 8:v.31

Then Yasodharā spoke, eyes red with anger,
her voice choking by the bitterness of despair,
her breast heaving with her sighs
tears streaming due to the depths of her grief:

v.32
"Chandaka where has that joy of my heart gone
leaving me as I slept helpless at night
As I see you and Kantaka return

---

3. I am using the translation by Patrick Olivelle from *Life of the Buddha* by Asvaghosa. Clay Sanskrit Library. New York: New York University Press, 2008. The quotations are from Canto 8.

when three had departed
my heart begins to tremble.

v.33
You have done me an ignoble, cruel and unfriendly act
so why do you weep here today you heartless man?
Contain your tears, be of good cheer!
your tears do not suit your deed!

. . .

v.35
It is better for a man to have a prudent foe
than a foolish friend, skilled in what is unfit:
For, calling yourself a friend, you fool
you have brought this family to great ruin."

Many centuries later, that anger resonates in a single verse of a Sri Lankan folk poet of the *Yasodharāvata* in the eighteenth or nineteenth century:

v.71
When the minister Canna returned to the city that day
The queen turned on him—a lioness leaping to the kill.
"Canna, friend, where is my loved lord today?
Go bring him to me now. I must see him. I will."

Again as Pajāpati Gōtami, his foster mother, laments in Ashvaghosa's poem, she refers to the rigors of the Bōdhisattva's ascetic life as contrasted with his past comforts.

v.55
Those soft feet of his, with lovely webbed toes,
tender like lotus fiber or a flower petal,
With concealed ankles, with whorls on the soles—
how will they tread on the rough forest ground?

v.56
Accustomed to sitting and lying on the palace terrace,
decked in priceless clothes, aloe, and sandal paste
How will his mighty body fare in the forest
amidst the cold the heat and the rains?

These same ideas surface in the work of the anonymous folk poet of Sri Lanka as part of Yasodharā's (not Gōtami's) lament.[4]

v.81
In the shadows of the forest you now walk,
There is no resting place for you in that dark.
Unceasing burns the fire that sears my heart,
My hand on my heart I beat my breast and weep.

v.98
My lord, on a bed of forest flowers are you sleeping?
Your tender lovely feet are they now hurting?
Are there sufficient gods around you, guarding?
Dear husband, my elephant king, where are you roaming?

As the Ashvaghosa poem indicates, Yasodharā's grief and her lament when she learns of her husband's departure, perhaps because it resonates with the popular tradition of folk laments in many cultures, is another point in the Yasodharā story that began very early to fire the imagination of poets and commentators and continued to do so over the centuries.

c) Yasodharā in the Mahāvagga

The *Mahāvagga*, another later canonical text, develops yet another incident. It is said that when the Buddha returned to his parental home of Kapilavastu after his Enlightenment to preach to his kinsmen, Yasodharā was absent. Some accounts say only that she refused to go with the rest of her family to hear her former husband, now the Buddha Gautama, preach. Other accounts also note that when she saw her husband, now a monk, begging for alms in the city street she pointed him out to her son and instructed him to go ask his father for his inheritance. The early texts do not expand on the implications of either action. Is there perhaps an element of residual hurt at a husband who abandoned her? Is there an implied criticism of an absent father in her request that he provide for his son? The questions are neither asked nor answered in the early Buddha narrative.

The *Mahāvagga*, however, does expand on the account of her first meeting with the Buddha after the seven-year separation and paints a poignant picture. The accounts give body to her presence only hinted at earlier and creating the

---

4. I quote from my translation of the anonymous Sinhala folk poem that is given in full in the next chapter.

popular perception of her as a woman of great devotion and strength of character. I quote from a translation by Paul Carus, of the text from the *Mahāvagga*.[5] The text states:

> Then the king conducted the prince into the palace and the ministers and all members of the royal family greeted him with great reverence, but Yasodharā, the mother of Rāhula, did not make an appearance. The king sent for Yasodharā, but she replied, "Surely if I am deserving of any regard, Siddhatta will come and see me." The Blessed One having greeted all his relatives and friends asked, "Where is Yasodharā?" And on being informed that she had refused to come he rose straightway and went to her apartments.
>
> "I am free" the Blessed One said to his disciples, Sāriputta and Moggallāna whom he had bidden to accompany him to the princess's chamber. "The princess however is not yet free. Not having seen me for a long time she is exceedingly sorrowful. Unless her grief is allowed its course her heart will cleave. Should she touch the Tathagata, the Holy One, you must not prevent her."
>
> Yasodharā sat in her room, dressed in mean garments and her hair cut. When the Buddha entered she was, from the abundance of her affection, like an overflowing vessel unable to contain her love. Forgetting that the man whom she loved was the Buddha, Lord of the World, the preacher of truth, she held him by his feet and wept bitterly. Remembering however that Suddhōdana was present she felt ashamed and rising, seated herself reverently at a distance.
>
> The king apologized for the princess saying, "This arises from her deep affection and is more than a temporary emotion. During the seven years that she had lost her husband when she heard that Siddhatta had shaved his head, she did likewise; when she heard that he had left off the use of perfumes and ornaments, she also refused their use. Like her husband she had eaten at appointed times from an earthen bowl only. Like him she had renounced high beds and splendid coverings and when princes asked her in marriage she replied that she was still his. Therefore grant her forgiveness."
>
> The Buddha spoke kindly to Yasodharā telling of her great Merits inherited from former lives. She had indeed been again and again of

---

5. *Mahāvagga*, Vol. XIII, verses 1–V, in *The Sacred Books of the East*. Oxford, 1881–1882, p. 18, quoted in Paul Carus, *Buddha, the Gospel*. Chicago: Open Court Publishing Co., 1894.

> great assistance to him. Her purity, her gentleness, her devotion had been invaluable to the Bōdhisattva when he aspired to attain Enlightenment, the highest aim of mankind. And so holy had she been that she desired to be the wife of a Buddha. This then was her *karma* and it is the result of great merit. Her grief has been unspeakable but the consciousness of the glory that surrounds her spiritual inheritance increased by her noble attitude during her life will be a balm that will miraculously transform all sorrows into heavenly joy.[6]

d) Bimbā's Lament in the Chengmai Text from Thailand

The incident described in the *Mahāvagga* is given a different turn in a much later prose version entitled "Bimbā's[7] lament" translated by Donald Swearer (in Lopez 1985) from a Thai text from Chengmai. I include it here as it provides yet another writer's perspective on Yasodharā's situation. The Thai folk account is described as "Yasodharā's lament" but is an interesting contrast to the lament in the Sinhala folk poem *Yasodharāvata* (The Story of Yasodharā), which I translate and discuss at length in chapter 1. Both laments, one in prose and one in verse, come from about the same period (probably between the eighteenth and nineteenth centuries) and both were probably reworkings of earlier versions. In the Sinhala version, Yasodharā's lament, as in the Ashvaghosa text, comes at the point when she first learns of her husband's departure to become a monk. In the Thai text, the lament is placed at the point when the Buddha returns to Kapilavastu to preach his doctrine to his father and kinsmen. In the Thai version, the lament is a complaint made to the servant who has come to convey her father-in-law's message that she should be present at the Buddha's preaching. An extract from this text follows:

> Having approached Bimbā, the servant paid her respects and asked "O queen why are you so sad and emaciated?" Bimbā looking at the maid replied, "O servant, come in. I shall tell you why I am so sorrowful nowadays. I am sad because the Lord Buddha, the founder of the religion no longer loves me even though I have done nothing wrong. I faithfully performed all my wifely duties toward him. I must be a person of little merit. I can accept being abandoned, but the Buddha should have sympathy for his son, Rāhula. He is lovable and innocent. His perfection is like that of a lotus standing above the surface of a pond. We have suffered greatly, as if crushed by a mountain.

---

6. Paul Carus. *Buddha, The Gospel.* Chicago: Open Court Publishing Co., 1894.

7. Bimbā is another name for Yasodharā.

> O my beloved Rāhula, You were a misfortune for your father from the very beginning. I have suffered as a widow; men look down on me; they do not respect me. A royal carriage is symbolized by its banner; a flame depends upon fire; a river exists because of the ocean; a state devoid of a ruler can not survive. Just so Rāhula, you and I having been abandoned are persons of no account. Everyone accuses you of being illegitimate; and people look down on me as a widow. My suffering brings only tears. How can I continue to live? I am ashamed before everyone. It is better for me to take poison and die or to put a rope around my neck and hang myself from the palace."
>
> Bimbā continued to sob uncontrollably.
>
> This transcriber then makes the following statement: "Here ends the first chapter of Bimbā's Lament. I copied this text in the afternoon of *Culasakarāja* 1161 (1799 CE) the year of the snake, the eleventh lunar month, the first day of the waning moon corresponding to the fifth day."[8]

The manuscript continues, however, suggesting the accretion of another version or text. Bimbā's complaint continues:

> My husband departed without even saying goodbye. He then returned unannounced and did not come to see me. In the past my Lord came to my quarters without telling anyone and came into my bedroom even when the bed was unmade. He was kind to me and was never harsh or angry. . . Now the Lord Buddha has come to see his father, but did not visit Bimbā, the mother of Rāhula . . . Though I, Bimbā, married a handsome lord I have truly suffered just like the old saying. This story will be told to future generations. O my servant I am not an evil person. This must be a consequence of evil *karma* in a past life. I'm like a tree that has lost its flowers and its fruit. I have been abandoned but not because of anything I have done.
>
> My Lord decided to take up the religious life and has reached enlightenment. Nothing that I have wanted has come to pass. My husband deserted me a long time ago and became a mendicant, leaving me filled with sorrow for the rest of my life.
>
> O servant, tell my father-in-law what I have said and that I, Bimbā, am unable to come to pay my respects. The king's son entered

---

8. Donald Swearer. "Bimbā's Lament." Buddhism in Practice, edited by Donald S. Lopez. Princeton: Princeton University Press, 1955.

> the court three days ago. My father-in-law did not send a servant to summon me . . . My lord was not gracious enough to come to my palace. The king knew the reason for this. I do not want to live anymore. O servant, please ask my father-in-law to forgive me." The servant took Bimbā's message to the king.[9]

This Thai prose text expresses the same fascination on the part of the author with the feelings of Yasodharā. The Thai version, however, is a more open complaint, a listing of grievances, and refers to aspects of social marginalization that probably went with widowhood and illegitimacy in the society of the time.

The Thai prose text, as with many other folk texts, indicates possible amalgamations and recompositions. Because palm leaf texts are a collection of loosely tied leaves (most often without any numbering), they can easily have their pages mis-collated. The placing of the events in the Chengmai Thai text suggests that this could have happened. I shall illustrate by isolating each event.

The details of the events described in the Chengmai text (only a part of which I have quoted) are in the following order:

1. Bimbā inquires about the excitement in the city. Is told her husband has returned. Is angry and humiliated that one who was once a prince now begs. She complains of desertion, sobs, and faints.
2. Regains consciousness, goes to the window, and sees the Buddha. There is then a long passage where she exclaims at length on the beauty of his person and points him out to her son. Then she goes to him, says she has come to pay her respects, falls at his feet, and worships him.
3. In a seeming reversal, in the next section she tells her father-in-law that in begging for alms "his actions disgrace and dishonor our family."
4. The king questions the Buddha on this point. The Buddha gives his reasons for doing so, and the king is converted.
5. The king sends for Bimbā. She makes a long complaint about the Buddha to the servant (section quoted earlier). She refuses to go to him. At this point, the scribe interjects and gives his identity, suggesting it is the end of a text.
6. The text resumes, goes back to the point where the servant conveys the king's request.

---

9. Ibid.

7. Bimbā continues her complaint. Tells the king she cannot come.
8. The king invites the Buddha to visit her.
9. On seeing the Buddha, Bimbā "felt angry and resentful." She falls at his feet "crying out her unhappiness."
10. Her sorrow slowly disappears. She regains composure, takes delight in the teaching and becomes a "Stream Enterer."

One realizes as one reads that perhaps two accounts of the incident have been incorporated into one by a (later) transcriber. The interpolation of one transcriber's identity that comes in the middle of the lament further confirms such amalgamation.

e) Yasodharā later in Mahayāna Sanskrit Texts

There are also the Mahayāna and Sanskrit traditions in which texts such as the medieval period Badrakalpavadāna and the Sanghabedhavastu section of the Sanskrit *Mūlasarvastivāda Vinaya* have even more elaborate stories of Yasodharā. They make no reference to the "great departure" which is so much a part of the Theravada tradition. Instead they expand on Yasodharā's life in the palace immediately before and after the departure of her husband. The accounts describe her relations with the Bōdhisattva on the night before his departure, the resulting conception, an extraordinary seven years of pregnancy that coincide with his seven year quest for enlightenment, and her sufferings and tribulations during the period of his absence. I make only a passing reference to these texts since they have been translated and commented on by other scholars such as John Tattleman[10] and John Strong.[11]

YASODHARĀ IN SINHALA LITERATURE

The Sinhala *Yasodharāpadānaya*[12] is a much expanded twelfth or thirteenth century version of the Pali *Yasodharāpadāna*. This text too deals with the events

10. John Tattleman, *The Trials of Yasodharā: A Critical Edition, Annotated Translation and Study of the Bhadrakalpavadāna*, Doctoral thesis submitted to Wolfson College, Oxford University, 1996.

11. John S. Strong, "A Family Quest: The Buddha, Yasodharā and Rāhula in the *Mūlasarvastivāda Vinaya*." *Sacred Biography in the Buddhist Traditions of South and Southeast Asia*, ed. Juliane Schobar. Honolulu: University of Hawaii Press, 1997.

12. *Yasodarāpadānaya* edited from the palm leaf manuscript B/5 at the Dharmagaveshana Parshadaya by the monk Dr. Meegoda Pannaloka Thēra and published in Colombo in 2000. The translation is mine.

associated with Yasodharā's final visit to the Buddha. She is now an *arahat* and goes to the Buddha for the ritual farewell performed by *arahats* before they die. There she recounts past lives in which she has been faithful to him amid all adversities and helped him in his quest for *nirvāṇa,* often sacrificing her life for him. The Buddha praises her exceptional devotion and meritorious actions throughout their journey together during uncountable numbers of existences in *saṃsāra.* He then requests her to display her supernormal powers as an *arahat* (which she has hitherto modestly hidden from the world) for the benefit of a public who have doubts about her being an *arahat.*

Because the Sinhala *Yasodharāpadānaya* is an important text of which there are many palm leaf manuscript versions still found in temple libraries in Sri Lanka, I have included a complete translation and comment on it in chapters 2 and 3.

Another very popular thirteenth century Sinhala work the *Pūjāvaliya* (Garland of Offerings)[1] treasured by generations of Sri Lankan Buddhists and repeatedly transcribed by successive generations of monks, has a chapter that expands even further on the *Yasodharāpadāna.* The writer incorporates much of the earlier *Yasodharāpadāna* material, but in Yasodharā's 'testimony' before the Buddha he adds material from other birth stories not included in the earlier Pali or Sinhala texts.

In a wonderful tour de force, with some ironic tongue-in-cheek comments, the author of the *Pūjāvaliya* has Yasodharā justify even her acts of cruelty toward the Bōdhisattva in a previous birth story familiar to Buddhists as the *Kusa Jātaka.*[14] I quote here a short section from the *Pūjāvaliya* to indicate how yet another author-monk in the thirteenth century brings in his own perspective on the character of Yasodharā. She says:

> For a long time in *saṃsāra* I lived united with you like your shadow. I was always faithful and supportive of you in all the different places we lived. However, women are frail and have little intellect. So you may at times find shortcomings [on my part]. But if you look with wisdom at each of these wrongs you will know that they did in fact help to strengthen your *pāramitā* (perfections or virtues needed to become a

---

13. Thera Mayurapada, *Pūjāvaliya.* Colombo: Gunasena and Sons, 1986, chapter 31, pp. 675–717.

14. In the *Kusa Jātaka,* the Bōdhisattva is born as the powerful but hideous King Kusa who falls in love with the extraordinarily beautiful princess Pabāvati. The story deals with her rejection of him and his determined wooing of her.

Buddha). Thus even wrongs done by me were in fact a source of benefit to you.

Leaving out other times, it is said that I treated you harshly in our *Kusa Jātaka* [existence]. You were then born as King Kusa and I as Pabāvati. At a time when I was intoxicated by my own beauty you disguised yourself and threw elephant dung and horse shit at me and sat on your elephant and made mocking gestures and faces at me and taunted me.[15] Then, even though I spoke abusively to you I did so in ignorance. Since there is no demerit in a non-volitional act I did no wrong.

When you hid in the royal pond and grabbed my hand saying, "I am King Kusa" how could I believe that a king could have a face like that—one that shamed the full moon in its [flat] ugliness. You who, in a past birth, had looked enviously at a Paccēka[16] Buddha when he was accepting an offering of flat cakes; because of that wrongful act you were born with an extremely repulsive face like a flat cake, terrifying all who saw it. "How can a king have a face like this? Surely it is a demon" I thought and mocked you as I would a demon. Therefore then too I was not to blame.

Thereafter I took my retinue, left [you, my husband] King Kusa and returned to my [natal] home. That too was a result of a fervent wish I had made in my past. Therefore I was again not to blame. [Pabavati then goes on to state how her actions, though at the time abusive and hurtful were in fact beneficial to the Bōdhisattva in that it enabled him to cultivate the ten virtues necessary to become a Buddha. She lists them one by one.]

"In that life, because of certain wrongs on my part, my husband in his devotion to me gave over his kingdom to his mother [in order to follow me] and in doing so perfected the virtue of Generosity (*dāna pāramitā*).

After you had won my affection in that life, because of your great love for me, you never sought other women and so observed the Five

---

15. The reference is to an incident when Kusa's handsome younger brother is paraded on the royal elephant to deceive Pabāvati and get her consent to the marriage with the ugly King Kusa. Meanwhile, Kusa, disguised as the elephant keeper, insults Pabāvati for her inordinate pride in her own beauty. She angrily abuses him for insulting her.

16. A *paccēka* Buddha is an enlightened being who, however, does not teach the Doctrine to others.

Precepts (*panca sīla*), thereby perfecting the virtue of Moral Conduct (*sīla pāramitā*).

In your devotion to me alone, in giving up your kingdom and traveling alone you perfected the virtue of Selflessness (*nekkhamma pāramitā*).

Learning different crafts [and skills] in order to create objects just for me, you perfected the virtue of Knowledge (*paññā pāramitā*).

In traveling four hundred leagues just to find me, you who lived the sheltered soft life of a king perfected the virtue of Effort (*vīriya pāramitā*).

Moreover, you who were king of all Dambadiva, instead of thinking, 'I will bring her back by force' bore me no ill will or anger. You bore with patience my angry words and thereby perfected the virtue of Kindness (*karuṇā pāramiṭā*).

"King Kusa, those who know how to make predictions will tell you that I will never be your wife. Your hope of getting me is like trying to get water to spring from a stone, or getting the wind to blow, or raising your hand to touch the moon. Do not expect to win me. Go back to your home," I said, deceptively. You said, "As I am a man I will certainly make you my chief queen [some day]. I will not go back to my kingdom without you" and in speaking so adamantly—words that you then later made come true—you perfected the virtue of Truth (*satya pāramitā*).

The [whirling] top you flung in one instant turned for fifteen hours and by your resolve you created various images of your forlorn love for me, for no other creature but me to see. So much so that even god Sakra's heaven was moved. You thereby perfected the virtue of Resolve (*adhittāna pāramitā*).

When seven enemy kings, ignorant of the kind of person you were, came seeking to marry [me] the chief queen of the king of all Dambadiva, you caught them and tied their hands with your shawl. But showing no anger at the time you let them go and even gave gifts of women. By that act you perfected the virtue of Compassion (*maitri pāramitā*).

In all those situations, unshaken, still as the mountain Mēru, by all you achieved you perfected the virtue of Equanimity (*upekkhā pāramitā*).[17]

---

17. *Pūjāvaliya* by Mayurāpada Thēra, extract from chapter 31. The translation is mine.

The woman who emerges from this text is not just the devoted wife and companion but a woman with a razor-sharp intellect who with almost legalistic acumen transforms negative material to make a positive case for herself. Each negative act she claims was beneficial in that it did propel the Bōdhisattva Kusa to perform the actions needed to fulfill each one of the Ten Perfections or *dasa pāramitā*.

The Sinhala folk poem *Yasodharāvata* (The Story of Yasodharā) written probably between the eighteenth and nineteenth centuries CE is another very popular poem on Yasodharā that has circulated in Sri Lanka for generations. Unlike many of the earlier commentarial texts, this is probably the work of a secular poet, not a monk. Its very human portrait of the woman Yasodharā has over the years become a part of the folk repertoire of Sinhala poetry. It is the text I have translated, and I shall refer to it hereafter as *Yasodharāvata* (A).[18]

There is another much later (perhaps late nineteenth century) Sinhala text called *Yasodharā Sāntiya* (Yasodharā: An Invocation for Blessings) in which the divine aspect created in the *Yasodharāpadāna* is further developed. In this poem she is treated as a deity and invoked to bring blessings to lay supplicants.

THE FOLK POEM *YASODHARĀVATA* (A)

It was only when I read the full text of the Sinhala *Yasodharāvata* (A) as an adult that I realized it was a long narrative poem with many verses totally unfamiliar to me. I had only known those verses called the lament (*vilāpaya*) that belonged to the popular folk repertoire. Perhaps for this reason, when reading the full text of the poem (as it exists today in its printed versions) I had a sense that it represented several strata accumulated over the years as different hands transcribed and shaped it.

The earliest written texts of the version that is popular today were transcribed on palm leaves, which is how Sri Lankan manuscripts were written and preserved until the popularization of printing in Sinhala in the early nineteenth century. Authorship unless stated in the body of a text was invariably anonymous, so texts could be expanded or contracted in the process of transcribing.

In the case of Sinhala folk poetry, additions can easily be made. Folk songs are generally composed in four-line end-rhymed stanzas. The four-line stanza has

---

18. S. Gamlath and E. A. Wickramasinghe, eds., *Yasodharāvata*. Colombo: Godage, 1995.

certain basic rhythmic patterns and the language lends itself easily to end rhymes. This makes additions to texts an easy task. Sinhala folk songs, for the most part, have a melancholic strain both in content and melody, perhaps because the villagers' recounting of the hardships of their world reflects the Buddhist worldview of contemplative resignation. Carters, while driving their bulls up steep hills or traveling at night along lonely roads, or farmers keeping watch in tree huts to keep at bay wild elephants and other marauders of their crops, compose such songs. They are an emotional expression of their hardships and experiences and also serve a more practical function by helping them to stay awake. The rhymed verses come easily.

Similarly, when women are transplanting or weeding rice fields and singing as they work, one will sing a verse and another will add to it, vary it, or compose a new verse to follow on. Still others will join in as a chorus, repeating a verse that has just been composed and thus adding new compositions to the already known repertoire. In a printed collection of folk songs published in the early years of the twentieth century there is one four-line stanza that gives an idea of how such compositions were made, and how they remained in circulation precisely because of such communal activities. I give a rough translation:

> Ran Ethana's voice fills out the cavern of her chest
> Punchi Menike sings from the *Yasodharāvata*
> Pathmavathi, little sister, listens to the song
> Others say, "Sing us the song of how weeding first began."[19]

The verse suggests that stanzas from the *Yasodharāvata* (A) were so familiar among villagers that when it is Punchi Menike's turn to sing a verse she sings one from the *Yasodharāvata.*

The tradition of funeral laments still extant in remote villages was another communal setting where such compositions were sung or chanted. The *vilāpaya* or lament section of the *Yasodharāvata* (A) was sung as a funeral lament in rural villages and would account for its familiarity with villagers. It is possible that the lament was extracted from the longer poem because of its emotional appeal. It is equally possible that the lament was the core to which later additions were made. I shall explore these possibilities when I discuss the different extant versions of the text later in the book.

---

19. J. M. Sala, ed., *Yasodharā Sinduva saha Satara Iriyavvē Sivpada.* Colombo: New Lanka Press, v. 61 (1949), p. 8.

One of the earliest extant Sinhala palmleaf manuscripts of a Yasodharā poem has a verse in the body of the text that states that the author was a woman, the eldest daughter of a minor king of the fourteenth century.[20] It is a totally different poem from the present-day popular folk poem the *Yasodharāvata* (A). It is significant however, that in this case authorship is claimed. Several other *Yasodharāvata* manuscripts often give the name of the transcriber, not the author. The act of transcribing was itself considered a meritorious act, so the practice was not unusual. However, this *Yasodharāvata* is one of the rare instances among extant prose and verse versions of the *Yasodharāvata*, where authorship is claimed—and by a woman—and so stated in the body of the text.

The *Yasodharāvata* (A) that I translate is an anonymous poem. It is titled the "Story of Yasodharā" but the biographical element is slight. The story line deals mainly with the life of the Bōdhisattva, not Yasodharā. The best known verses of the poem, however, are the lament of Yasodharā over the departure of her husband. A good part of the rest of the poem also deals with feminine concerns—the dreams of childbirth of the mother of the Bōdhisattva, and her pregnancy cravings—all described at some length, and give it a feminine perspective, even if one cannot claim a feminine author for this particular poem.

THE TRADITION OF LAMENT IN SINHALA POETRY

The *Yasodharāvata* (A) is today both a popular folk poem and sung as a funeral lament. The tradition of lament is not unfamiliar to folk societies and goes back in time. Laments have been described as "texted performances of grief conventionally required in many societies at funerals" by James M. Wilce who worked in Bangladesh.[21] It can sometimes take the form of an individual lament for the loss of a loved one as in the Old English poem, "The Wife's Lament" composed, scholars believe, around the ninth or early tenth century in England.[22] It can also take the form of communal mourning at a death of a loved one or close

---

20. K. D. Somadasa, ed. *The Catalogue of the Hugh Neville Collection of Sinhala Manuscripts in the British Library*, vol. 3. London: Pali Text Society, 1990, p. 164. See also appendix A.

21. James M. Wilce, "Genres of Memory and the Memory of Genres: Forgetting, Lament in Bangladesh," *Comparative Studies in Society and History*, 44: 159–185.

22. Jane Chance, *Woman as Hero in Old English Literature*. Syracuse, NY: Syracuse University Press, 1986, pp. 81–94.

kinsman. In the latter case, the lament comprises of both patterned formalized expressions of grief as well as interjections of more personal experiences.

Different cultures may structure this balance differently. Isabel Nabokov[23] has a detailed account of funeral laments in a rural South Indian village where the laments follow a traditional pattern, but the interpolations are of an extremely personal nature. In the remote village of Laggala in central Sri Lanka, where even as late as the 1950s formal doctrinal Buddhism had only begun to make inroads, laments were a common expression of mourning at funerals. They consisted of chanted verses interrupted by certain standard exclamations uttered loudly, such as, "Alas, my child is gone!" "O when will I ever see him again!," accompanied by standard gestures like breast-beating or holding one's head with one hand and swaying up and down. The formal laments could be interjected, however, with completely mundane statements like "Give that visitor a chair" or "Has the rice been brought from next door?" and the lament would resume with the very next breath.

Verses of lament from folk poems such as the *Yasodharāvata* (A) and the *Vessantara Kāvya* are generally chanted by groups of villagers seated at night around the body of a dead person awaiting burial. In the former, a wife mourns the loss of her husband. In the latter, a mother, the wife of Vessantara, mourns the loss of her young children. Among the Catholic communities in the coastal area of western Sri Lanka, laments still form so important a feature of funerals that mourners are hired to 'perform' them. In such situations, as with the case of "skilled cry women" in Finland[24] "who could safely deliver souls to Tuonela—the world of the dead"—the lament is more ritualized and its content more standardized.

It is possible, since laments are so widespread an expression of mourning in folk societies around the world, that in Sri Lanka too the lament (*vilāpaya*) may have been of pre-Buddhist origin. Its inclusion in a Buddhist framework is likely to have been a natural development once Buddhism took root in the society. There is the other possibility that, like so many other cultural exchanges between Sri Lanka and South India over the centuries, the tradition of lament was introduced through somewhat later South Indian contact.

Today, however, the modern Buddhist stress on the doctrinal attitude to death has resulted in a shift in the manner of mourning and the elimination of

---

23. Isabel Nabokov, *Religion Against the Self: An Ethnography of Tamil Rituals*. Berkeley: University of California Press, 2000.

24. Tolbert (1944), 91. Quoted in J. M. Wilce, "Genres of Memory and the Memory of Genres: Forgetting, Lament in Bangladesh," op. cit.

vilāpa at Buddhist funerals. *Vilāpa* or laments may still be a feature of funerals in rural Sri Lanka, but even there the beating of breasts and the loud exclamations seem to be giving way to the more formal communal chanting of verses. These verses are still sometimes from folk poems like the *Yasodharāvata* (A), but now, increasingly, they are verses from certain Buddhist Pali *suttas* (stanzas from the canon). Even that practice is dying out in urban parts of the country where women's weeping is subdued and grief is expressed with ever more "protestant Buddhist"[25] restraint.

The existence of several other popular laments in Sinhala poetry suggests that the tradition may have been much more pervasive in earlier times. One such lament is associated with the rituals for the goddess Pattini that are thought to have come to Sri Lanka from Southern India.[26] There is a section in the *Pattini Hälle* (The Tale of Pattini) where the goddess finds her husband killed by the evil king of Madurai and chants verses of lament as she weeps over his dead body. Her *vilāpaya* (verses of lament), sung by the ritual specialist dressed in female clothes, enacting the role in the ritual arena, are some of the most moving verses in the Pattini rituals.

Similarly, there is the lament of Kuveni, in the *Kuveni Hälle* (The Tale of Kuveni). She was the legendary queen of the island before the introduction of Buddhism. When Prince Vijaya, the mythical ancestor of the Sinhala race, came to the island from India, he met Kuveni, married her, and was made by her the ruler of the island. Vijaya later sought to legitimize his rule by bringing high caste 'queens' from India as wives for himself and his men and banished Kuveni from his court. The lament of the banished Kuveni is a complaint against this act of desertion and broken faith.

In the *Vessantara Kāvya* (Poem of Vessantara), the Bōdhisattva, in his life as King Vessantara, seeks to perform the Act of *Dāna* (generous giving) by not refusing any request made to him. He gives away his kingdom, all material possessions, and, when asked, even gives away his two young children. The most moving and best known verses in the poem are those describing the lament of Madri Devi, the wife of the Bōdhisattva Vessantara, as she mourns the loss of her two young children. She combs the forest looking for them and accosts the wild creatures that live there for information about her missing children.

---

25. The term is now used to describe the transformations that took place in early twentieth century interpretations of Buddhist doctrine influenced by Colonel Olcott and Anagarika Dharmapala.

26. Gananath Obeyesekere, *The Cult of the Goddess Pattini*. Chicago: University of Chicago Press, 1974.

Though laments may go back to a much earlier pre-Buddhist tradition of mourning, scholars believe that the *Kuveni Hälle*, the *Yasodharāvata* (A), and the *Vessantara Kāvya* in the forms in which they exist today, were composed during what historians refer to as the Kandy period in Sinhala literary history (seventeenth to early nineteenth centuries). The kings of Kandy then still controlled the central areas of the island, even though the coastal areas were under Western colonial control. Many of the verses of the *Yasodharāvata* (A) use vocabulary and speech patterns found even today among villagers in the Kandyan area. The inclusion of long laments, however, within the body of what would otherwise be a narrative poem suggests that the tradition of laments may have an older origin.

In all these laments, the narrative persona, if not the actual author of the poem, is a woman. Yasodharā, Kuveni, Pattini, and Madri Devi are all women faced with loss. The laments are therefore the expression of loss in very feminine terms. They are often embedded in a larger narrative that provides a context for the lament, but it is these verses that are excerpted and sung especially at funerals and are therefore the most popular and best known sections of the poems.

The tradition of laments may have come from India or may have had pre-Buddhist origins, but the Sri Lankan laments referred to are now very much a part of a Buddhist tradition or have been incorporated into that tradition. Therefore, while being expressions of grief over a loss, they also express resignation and acceptance of what Buddhists believe to be a necessary condition of *samsāric* existence. The core verses that form the lament in the poem *Yasodharāvata* (A) are sung at rural funerals in order to help mourners achieve that acceptance. The verses speak of grief and loss, but there is also an emotional progression, a slow movement toward resignation and final acceptance of a situation that cannot be changed or reversed, a loss that cannot be recovered. It is perhaps this sense of finality—such as comes from Yasodharā's knowledge that her husband Siddharta will not, cannot, ever come back to her as her husband—that makes the verses of her lament both a powerful vehicle for grief as well as an acceptance of and resignation to loss. The Buddhist resignation, the hard but necessary acceptance of the inevitability of the parting, is what enables the singing of the verses to bring solace to mourners.

THE *YASODHARĀVATA* (A) IN THE CONTEXT OF SINHALA LITERARY HISTORY

The Early Period

Sinhala literature has a long history. The earliest extant works that have survived come from about the seventh century CE, but the tradition goes back much further to about the third century BCE. This very early literature consisted for the most part of Buddhist religious writings or accounts of kings who supported Buddhism. That early literature is now lost, but evidence from extant Pali and Sanskrit sources such as the fourth and sixth century Sri Lankan chronicles, the *Dīpavaṃsa* and the *Mahavaṃsa*, composed in Pali from existing Sinhala sources, and the colophons to fifth century Pali translations such as the *Dhammapadaṭṭhakathā* that claim as their source earlier Sinhala works, indicate the existence of such a literature.

What has been preserved of early Sinhala literature (until about the twelfth century CE) is essentially a religious literature, the work mainly of scholar monks, preserved by them and strongly influenced by the classical Sanskrit and Pali traditions with which they were familiar. There was very likely also a secular literature at the time, but such manuscripts were probably of no importance to the monks and not preserved in temple libraries. The existence of a body of graffiti poems scribbled on the wall of the rock fortress at Sigiriya and dating from between the seventh and the eleventh centuries CE suggests, however, that such a secular literature did exist.[27]

Between the tenth and twelfth centuries, Sinhala literature was strongly influenced by the Sanskrit classical tradition and even the language became heavily Sanskritized. From the thirteenth to the fifteenth centuries, however, there was a move away from the Sanskritic influences of earlier classical scholarship, and what might be termed an intermediate literary tradition developed. The works preserved from this period were still mainly religious and composed by monks, but the style had changed. The writings, especially the prose, began to reflect the language used in popular sermons for lay audiences. They were still written in a formal style, but less heavily classicist and closer to colloquial speech, with images drawn from daily life. The *Saddharmaratnāvaliya* (Jewel Garland of the True Doctrine), the *Pūjāvaliya* (Garland of Worship), and the *Butsaraṇa* (Refuge in the Buddha) are three major works that belong to this tradition.

Between the sixteenth and nineteenth centuries, two fairly distinct styles can be distinguished in the literature. One was that of the classical writings of the scholarly tradition and the other was that of a secular literature of both prose and poetry written in a more colloquial form, composed by a local intelligentsia writing for a more popular readership. The popularity of these secular works meant that they soon passed into the folk repertoire and several versions and variations were introduced. Though the authorship of these secular writings is

27. Senarat Paranavitana, *The Sigiri Graffiti*, London: Published for the Government of Ceylon by Oxford University Press, 1956.

for the most part unclaimed, they belong to a genre that was often the work of individual authors. Many of them were written down, though we do not know whether by the authors themselves or by later scribes. Several have been found in palm leaf manuscript collections.

The secular poetry of this period was most often composed in four-line, end-rhymed stanzas. The vocabulary was simple, almost colloquial, and the images often repetitive and from a stock repertoire. The metrical patterns were the familiar ones enabling the verses to be sung or chanted. Rules of grammar and syntax were not necessarily always followed, and the end rhymes were sometimes forced. All these features were conducive to a form of storytelling in verse that became quite popular during this period.

These *vaṃsakatā* (narrative poems) of the secular literature were distinct from the body of religious literature written mainly by monks, transcribed and retranscribed by monks, and preserved in temple libraries over the centuries. The *vaṃsakatā* dealt with matters of more secular interest, historical events, battles, heroic individuals, or poetic retellings of popular narratives. They were composed most often by laypeople and transcribed by them—as the semiskilled quality of some of the palm leaf scripts suggest. Many of these poems or sections of them were probably transcribed onto palm leaves by local intelligentsia and not necessarily by the authors or at the time they were composed. Many were also preserved in family collections. There are several categories of these narrative poems. There are the *hatan kavi* (battle poems) such as the *Ingrīsi hatana* (Battle against the English). There are *vitti kavi* (poems of events) that recount some tragic or historic event such as the *Ähälepola Kāvya* (which relates the tale of the killing of the children of Ähälepola on the orders of the king). There are love poems such as the *Dunuwila hatana* (about the amorous exploits of a chieftain named Dunuwila), or narrative poems based on religious stories from the *Jātakas* or Buddhist legends. These were all composed in the popular style, often by laymen and women rather than by monks. There are also individual poems by named authors, such as those of the women poets Gajaman Nona and Ranchagoda Hamine.

These secular poems became very popular. Sometimes the original authors were forgotten, but their poems were sung, handed down, sometimes also written down in palm leaf manuscripts, and finally became part of the folk repertoire.[28]

28. The *Ingrīisi hatana* has been attributed to the authorship of Veligalle Rala in the eighteenth century. An early version of the the *Yasodharāvata* is claimed to have been written by the eldest daughter of Bopiti nirindu—a minor king of the fourteenth century. Both are also considered anonymous folk poems.

The *Yasodharāvata* (A) and the *Vessantara Kāvya* belong to this last category. Both poems recount an already familiar event from the Buddha stories, but both have as their central interest the laments of the two women faced with loss. In the *Yasodharāvata* (A), Yasodharā mourns the departure of her husband. In the *Vessantara Kāvya*, Madri Devi the mother mourns the loss of her children. It is on abandonment and emotional desolation that the secular poets expand—a theme hardly touched on in the stories as they appear in the religious Buddha narrative of monks. The emotional intensity implicit in the situations no doubt triggered the imagination of secular poets and gave rise to verses that appealed to the experiences of ordinary people.

The Colonial Period

Sri Lanka had begun to feel the impact of colonial encroachment as early as the sixteenth century. The Portuguese from 1505 to 1648, then the Dutch from 1648 to 1776, and the British from 1776 to 1815, in turn captured and colonized Sri Lanka's coastal area. All these foreign powers, however, had control only of a section of the country. Native rulers controlled the interior, and so the Buddhist religion and Sinhala literature continued to be patronized by kings and scholars and Buddhist religious works were fostered by the monks and preserved in monasteries. After 1815, however, when the British finally took control of the entire island, the situation changed dramatically. Patronage of the religion (Buddhism) and the native language of the majority of the people (Sinhala) soon ceased, and the colonial establishment set about introducing English as the language of government, and Christianity as the favored religion. Acceptance ensured upward mobility for Sri Lankans and entrance into the lower echelons of the colonial administration.

As a result, one section of the local intelligentsia was slowly absorbed into the colonial English-speaking part of society, was taught to look down on the native language, and ceased to write in Sinhala. The classical works, wherever possible, were preserved by monks in village temples, but remained mostly unread. Over time, these works became almost unintelligible to the lay public. The Sinhala language also began to reflect a significant break. The literary language of classical scholarship remained fixed while the colloquial language spoken by the less sophisticated sections of society changed quickly.

The creative work extant from this period belongs to the secular tradition that had come down from the seventeenth and eighteenth centuries. It is a form of popular poetry, often anonymous, composed by villagers expressing the concerns and hardships of their world, or narratives of events, or of individual lives composed by sections of the rural intelligentsia. Most of these poems were sung or chanted and intended to be so. Their popularity arose from the fact that, though they may have been written down in palm leaf manuscripts, they were also handed down orally. Like all oral literature, they were subject to changes in the recitation and in the transference. Many of the works thus came to be seen as anonymous, and scribes who felt a need to record them also felt free to make changes to the works as they thought fit.

The popular style of these poems, the four-lined end-rhymed stanza, depended for its effect on alliteration, internal rhymes, puns, and melodic patterning. Sometimes a four-line, end-rhymed stanza was intended to stand as an individual poem. In such cases, compression resulted in highly nuanced and suggestive images that set up reverberations of meaning. I give here my attempt at translating such a four-lined love poem.

Taksalāva sanda mudunen tiyen nā
Duksalāva sita yata kärakäven nā
Malvelāva baṃbarun rōnata en nā
Makvelāda ada mata nidi noyen nā

Taxila[29] lies far beyond the moon
A whirlpool of grief churns deep beneath my mind.
Bees come for honey when it's flowering time
Why is it sleep comes not to me, tonight?

The first line conjures up a world of youth, scholarship, and perhaps love associated with the famous Buddhist university of Taxila. The next line suggests tormenting grief at the loss of that world and, more personally, a lost love that the third and fourth lines clearly confirm. The simple Sinhala of the verse with its internal rhymes, alliteration and patterning is extremely powerful and moving.

Longer narrative poems like the *Yasodharāvata* (A), often based on a known story, were in similar stanza form but joined together by a narrative thread. The language and imagery were more standard, drawn from a known repertoire, and the poetic power came more from the manner in which the emotional events were handled and retold than in the originality or intrinsic power of the images.

John Davy,[30] an Englishman writing in the early nineteenth century, comments that in Sri Lanka at the time, not only was there a high rate of literacy but

29. Taxila was a famous seat of scholarship located in northwest India, but a place name familiar to Sri Lankans as a seat of Buddhist learning.

30. John Davy, *An Account of the Interior of Ceylon and of Its Inhabitants with Travels in That Island.* London, 1821; republished in Colombo, Tissara Pyakashakyo Press, 1983, p. 176–177.

that "almost every Singalese is more or less a poet; or at least can compose what they call poetry." The remark stems no doubt from the fact that most people could compose a four-line end-rhymed stanza and many did—though not all could claim to be poets.

I make passing mention here of the tradition of chants or narrative poems of the origin myths of gods and demons, sung by ritual specialists or shamans in rituals to propitiate such deities and exorcise evil spirits. These chants are familiar only to the families of ritual specialists and handed down by them to their descendants or pupils. The tradition is mostly oral, but occasionally there are claims that they exist in the form of written texts (jealously guarded by the shaman families). There is a considerable body of such poetry (some of it very beautiful) coming down from perhaps the sixteenth or seventeenth century and commonly sung in performances in the villages. However, perhaps because such ritual chants were considered extraneous to the Theravada Buddhist tradition (carefully preserved by monks), they have not been seen as part of the Sinhala literary tradition, even by present-day lay scholars and literary historians. Only anthropologists have so far evinced interest in this body of poetry and while some small portion of it has been recorded by them, most of it will soon be lost to posterity with the dying of the rituals and their specialists.

The Religious, Literary, and Nationalist Revival of the Late Nineteenth Century

By the late nineteenth century, there was a powerful anticolonialist, nationalist Buddhist resurgence. One of its expressions was a revival of native literature. Fuelled by the availability of printing, classical literary works that had been preserved in palm leaf manuscripts in Buddhist monasteries were collected, edited, and printed for a public of classical scholars.

Around the same time, there was a spate of publications of cheaper editions in the form of pamphlets and booklets of folk poems and popular narrative poetry. These were sold in the marketplace for an avid local reading public. They were very different from the formal, stylized, and now almost incomprehensible language of the classical literary works. These *kavi kola*, or pamphlet poems as they came to be called, were treated as anonymous and published in cheap editions for quick sale. Sellers of these pamphlets sang them out loud in the marketplace in their attempts to gather an audience and hawk their wares. Crowds often gathered round to listen, and the booklets had an instant market. Printed publications gave a fixed or definitive form to the poems that up to then had been subject to changes and variations in oral transmission. Once printed, the texts became fairly consistent and differed only slightly in the many versions. Thus, today there are several versions of the *Yasodharāvata* (A) poem, many of them still in pamphlet form, but a comparison of several such 'texts' provides only a few not very significant variations. The sellers of these pamphlets in the marketplace have almost disappeared today. The pamphlets can still be found, occasionally, among pavement booksellers, and at pilgrimage centers, but, even so, takers are few.

THE PRINTED TEXTS

Many printed 'pamphlet' versions of the *Yasodharāvata* exist.[31] They vary little from the popular poem *Yasodharāvata* (A). The earliest extant printed copies in the National Museum Library at Colombo are both dated 1894; one contains 124 verses, the other 130 verses. Neither is very different from *Yasodharāvata* (A), though they begin and end at different points in the poem, which perhaps makes for a significant difference.

Of these two texts of *Yasodharāvata* in the National Museum Library in Sri Lanka, the one dated 1894 consists of 124 verses written by M. D. R Appuhamy and I will call this text *Yasodharāvata* B or Y(B). The other, also dated 1894, consists of 130 verses and I will call it *Yasodharāvata* C or Y(C). What is significant is that version Y(B) starts exactly as my translated version, but ends with what is verse 124 in the *Yasodharāvata* (A) text. It does not have the exhortation to women embodying the patriarchal values with which *Yasodharāvata* (A) concludes—verses 125–130. The break is significant because that is a section which even on a first reading seemed to be clearly the addition of another layer to the poem. The name of the writer, M. D. R. Appuhamy, who was probably transcribing a poem he knew, suggests that he belonged to the traditional literati of the village and was familiar with village folk songs.

The text Y(C), though published the same year, is different. It was published by the Buddhist Publication Society, edited by G. C. M. Suriya, and does contain the exhortation to women to be subservient and obey their husbands in all things. The Buddhist Publication Society was set up to promote a modern interest in Buddhism by the publication of Buddhist texts and commentaries. Colonel Olcott and Anagarika Dharmapala were two key figures associated with this movement. It was a revivalist as well as a modernist movement to encourage a new Buddhism to fit in with the demands of modern nationalist and (anti) colonial society. But, in doing so, it introduced certain values that were seen as

31. A discussion of the palm leaf manuscripts appears in the appendix. I deal here only with the printed pamphlet texts.

non-Western because they were drawn from Hindu India, but that dovetailed nicely with the Victorian puritan values (that had seeped into the society after colonial contact and were at the time) regarded as modern. Some of the books published by the Buddhist Publications Society, intended as nationalist revivalist works, disseminated these patriarchal values. The *Yasodharāvata* as published by this society then became the standard version of the poem. It is this text that was republished repeatedly in pamphlet form for sale at markets and fairs.

No doubt, there are many other pamphlet versions of the *Yasodharāvata* printed well into the twentieth century, but most of them vary only very slightly—just an occasional word —from the text I have used for my translation, which has now come to be the 'fixed' text. The catalogue of the Sri Lankan National Museum Library records two other pamphlet publications dated 1885 and 1887, but they are missing.

The *Yasodharāvata* (A) that I have translated is considered an anonymous folk poem. The edition I decided to use was by Dr. Sucharitha Gamlath and E. A. Wickramasinghe. It was published in Colombo in 1995 by Godage Brothers, and reprinted in 1998 and 2001. The poem consists of 130 verses with a critical introduction.

Of two other tattered 'pamphlet' versions I own, one is entitled *Yasodharāvata*, is anonymous, and is published by A. S. De Silva at the Gunasekera printers in Aluthgama. I shall call it Y(D). There is no date of publication. The cover, a picture of a Madonna-style Queen Māyā with the Bōdhisattva on her lap, both surrounded by halos (could also be intended for Yasodharā sitting with Rāhula on her lap), suggests that it was possibly printed in the late nineteenth or early twentieth century when such Christian iconography had become familiar to the culture. The text is almost identical to the *Yasodharāvata* (A) with only a few minor word changes that I have not considered worth noting. A poem as popular as the *Yasodharāvata* had many printed pamphlet versions, but the text, once fixed in print, did not permit too much variation—unlike the palm leaf manuscripts of earlier times.

The second pamphlet Y(E) is entitled *Yasodharā Sinduva* (Song of Yasodharā) and consists of fifty-two verses. It is a collection put together by G. M. Sala and published by K. A. Dineshami at the Lankābhinava Press in 1949. What I have is the fifth edition, so the first edition may have been printed in the early years of the century. The cover picture is of Yasodharā in a saree (the style introduced from India in the late nineteenth century) seated in a Victorian-style chair, in conversation with the Minister Canna who is dressed in what seems a vaguely Indian garb. The caption reads, "The Minister Canna conveys news to Queen Yasodharā that Prince Siddharta has become a monk."

The first thirty-eight verses of this version describe the birth and early life of the Bōdhisattva up to the point of his departure and Canna's return to inform Yasodharā that he has gone. Yasodharā's lament that follows is confined to eight verses (39–46). Though less elaborate, the themes are almost identical to those in the other versions. The next set of verses (47–51) describe events during the Enlightenment, the Buddha's subsequent preaching, and his death. The last verse (52) relates that Yasodharā becomes a nun, dies, and achieves *nirvāṇa*. The verse form is the four-line, end-rhymed stanza, the events described are the same, but the verses are completely different and suggest they may have come from a different source. The pamphlet also contains a collection of other folk poems sung when transplanting and weeding rice fields.

AN ANALYSIS OF THE POEM *YASODHARĀVATA* (A)

My close reading of the poem *Yasodharāvata* (A) and a study of the palm leaf and other manuscript versions tend to suggest a text composed of several strata. A kind of poetic stratigraphy or layering seems to have taken place. The first 117 verses read as a clearly narrative poem beginning with the story of the Bōdhisattva's birth and ending with the death of Yasodharā. This I believe is the basic text of the poem *Yasodharāvata* (A). The emphasis on the dreams of childbirth of Queen Māyā, her pregnancy cravings after she conceives, and the verses of lament by Yasodharā when her husband leaves her—all present very feminine concerns and might even suggest a feminine author.

Verses 118–124 mark a sharp and definite change in rhythm and meter, tone and content. The lines are long and are in a tone of invocation very similar in form and metrical patterning to verses sung by shamans in exorcist or healing rituals or in formal invocations to the deities. They refer to magical powers and superhuman acts attributed to Yasodharā. She is viewed as a powerful deity, an aspect that is elaborated in the *Yasodharāpadāna* manuscripts (composed perhaps by monks) but less well known at the folk level. This aspect of Yasodharā's power seems to be a later addition. It is possible that a monk engaged in the process of transcribing, aware of the accounts in the commentaries such as the *Yasodharāpadānaya*, decided to add this section to the poem.

The final verses (125–130, six stanzas) mark yet another shift in tone, content, and sensibility. This section is a moralistic homily and seems even more clearly the addition of yet another strata to the poem. It is a sermon to women embodying explicit patriarchal values—a moral exhortation. In the late nineteenth century and early twentieth century, such values on gender and feminine roles began to influence and slowly seep into Sinhala society. Their impact was most intense in the latter years of the nineteenth century and in the first half of the twentieth century with the Buddhist reform movement that spread rapidly among the middle classes.[32] This last section of the *Yasodharāvata* (A) as it is now found in printed versions seems to belong to this period. One of the palm leaf manuscripts (see the appendix) seems to confirm that this section was probably added when the poem went into print at the end of the nineteenth century. I shall substantiate my reading of the poem by the following analysis of its narrative structure.

The *Yasodharāvata* (A) is titled the *Story of Yasodharā*, but there is little biographical information on Yasodharā. The core and the best known section of the poem is the lament of Yasodharā over the departure of her husband, the single most searing event in her life. Thirty verses express Yasodharā's lament at the loss of a beloved husband, her sense of abandonment, her inability to comprehend why her husband left without telling her when she had always supported him in his quest for Buddhahood, and her desperate efforts to come to terms with the finality of his departure, to understand and accept the larger cause that made her husband pursue the course he did. They form the poignant core of the poem and are the feelings of any woman/every woman. Their powerful human appeal has made the poem justly popular among generations of Sri Lankans

In the folk imagination of Sinhala Buddhists, the poem *Yasodharāvata* has always been a poem of love and loss, despair and resignation, and ultimately equanimity born of acceptance. It is framed within the context of the Buddha story, but, while the narrative is important, it is cursorily given not just because the story is familiar to readers or listeners but because the folk poet's interest, as the title suggests, centers on the woman Yasodharā.

The *Yasodharāvata* (A) begins with a brief account of the Bōdhisattva's interminable journey in *saṃsāra*. It describes the prophecies made by earlier Buddhas about him as well as his decision to leave the heavenly kingdom of the gods to come once more to earth in order to become a Buddha and show humans the path to escape suffering. This long space of infinite *saṃsāric* time, counted in *asankya* (uncountables) and *kalpa* (eons) is compressed into nine verses (1–9).

The scene then shifts to Queen Māyā, destined to be the mother of the Bōdhisattva. Twenty-one verses (10–30) describe her prophetic dreams about the

---

32. See the scholarship on the impact of Anagarika Dharmapala and the Buddhist revivalism in the work done by scholars such as S. Ammunugama, K. Malalgoda, G. Obeyesekere, and H. L. Seneviratne.

child to be born to her; once conception has occurred, they describe her pregnancy cravings. The dreams and the description of the pregnancy cravings are all part of accepted Buddhist lore regarding the birth of the Bōdhisattva. However, the anonymous poet deals with them at length, in elaborate detail. By contrast, the birth, early life, and marriage of the Bōdhisattva until the moment of the *abhinikmana* (the Great Renunciation) are given in a rapid summary of six verses (33–38). It is significant that twenty-one verses are allotted to describe Queen Māyā's dreams and cravings during her pregnancy while twenty-nine years of the Bōdhisattva's early life are summed up in a cryptic account of less than ten verses.

The scene shifts again to the moment when the Bōdhisattva, about to leave for a life of asceticism, is told the news of the birth of his son. In the story familiar to Theravada Buddhists, this is a very poignant moment of crisis in the Bōdhisattva's life. He goes to see his wife and newborn son, is about to enter but does not, pauses on the threshold, steps back, turns, and leaves. The *Yasodharāvata* poet elaborates on this moment. In ten verses (43–52) the poet expresses the conflicting pull. On the one side is his love and concern for a wife who has given him unstinting love and support throughout their *saṃsāric* existences. There is the attraction of her beauty, the human bonds that draw him to his first sight of his first child, and the strong desire to speak to his wife before he leaves. Against this is the self-knowledge that he must leave without allowing himself even that minimal luxury if he is to keep his resolve to strive for Buddhahood. Some of the most beautiful and often quoted verses in the poem are the simple description of the sleeping queen and her son. It is impossible to capture the softness expressed in the alliteration of 's' sounds in the following verse (61):

Sōma guṇa sisila simḅa sanasana muhu na[33]
Pēma guṇa sobana kumarun vadā gena
Pun sanda langa sitina ran tharuvak lesi na
Pun sanda men vaditi kumarun sihi kara na.

Her gentle face that soothes with soft kisses
The lovely child held closely in her arms
Is a golden star that shines beside a full moon.
Like a moon he leaves now, thinking of his son.

The Bōsat's lingering silent farewell to his wife and child, along with his resolution and irresolution, are expressed in verses 46–50.

33. *simḅa sanasana* (soothe with kisses) has a soft 's' sound used alliteratively for the entire line.

From long ago I fulfilled all the Virtues
I practiced 'giving' to be a Buddha, to save all beings.
She is lovely, moon-like, pre-eminent among women—
Shall I say one word to my dear queen?

My lovely queen sleeps on her golden bed.
Shall I draw near look at my baby by her side?
Her arm cradling him is a golden vine,
My eyes are drawn to my lovely sleeping queen.

The baby sucks his milk from that jeweled dome.
What more is there to see, what is the use?
You never failed me, not in thought or deed.
His mind holds firm, his eyes fill with tears.

You've wept more tears for me than the seas hold water
Does this wide world hold a woman as good as you?
Today I leave you in order to become a Buddha.
I must destroy desire, be firm in my resolve.

For one wife and one child do I give up my quest
Or save countless creatures from the *saṃsāric* round?
No, today I'll leave all I love, become an ascetic.
What an amazingly lovely child is my Rāhula!

It is the folk poet's ability to create a human portrait of the Bōdhisattva, torn between the decision to leave the palace and his human ties of love for his wife and newborn child, that gives balance to the poem. Otherwise Yasodharā's long and despairing lament and reproaches that follow soon after would seriously undermine the Buddhist worldview of the total poem by presenting the Bōdhisattva's act as one of heartless cruelty.

The emotional balance of the poem comes from the interplay between the two parallel sections in the narrative poem. One describes the pain of parting the Bōdhisattva feels as he goes to see his sleeping wife and newborn son before his final departure, and the other depicts Yasodharā's grief at his departure. Their individual expressions of pain and grief exemplify very human emotions—a man determined to leave those he loves for a higher cause and a woman's sense of abandonment and despair at the loss of a loved husband. Yasodharā's grief is exacerbated by what she sees as a breach of trust. After all the years they spent together in *saṃsāra* when she had helped her husband in his efforts to reach this goal, he has now left without telling her. Again and again the verses come back to this reproach. At this point, the readers' knowledge (from the earlier verses in the poem) that the Bōdhisattva left without waking her because he was himself too human and unsure of the power of his own emotions, helps the reader to modify criticism of the Bōdhisattva. The Bōdhisattva has to leave without a word to her because the ties of passion are still strong and he is still very human. He must leave without waking her if he is to keep to his resolve and find a solution to the suffering of mankind. Yasodharā's own grief, however, is also tempered by her continuing love and her equally human, womanly concern for the welfare of the beloved. This concern enables her finally to come to terms with her loss.

The Buddhist worldview is also strengthened by the description of Yasodharā's grief as process—a forward movement from her first almost manic attack on Canna, whom she tries to hold responsible for her husband's departure, to a mood of resignation and acceptance as she turns to a life of Buddhist meditation. Slowly, the poet leads us beyond the recurring question—why did you leave without a word to me? Yasodharā's grief is not anger at his departure. She has known from the beginning that to be a Buddha was his goal and she has shared his life and his efforts toward that goal in all their past existences in *saṃsāra*. She has done so with a full knowledge of what it means. What she cannot understand is that on this one occasion he has gone leaving her behind, alone, and without a word to her. It is as an answer to this recurrent question that the poet's account of the Bōdhisattva's hesitations, his human ambivalences and desires, takes on significance. They help to modify what might otherwise seem cruelty on his part and legitimate reproach on hers.

For Yasodharā, as she goes through the formal patterns of lament, remembering their past lives in *saṃsāra*, recounting the many times when they did things together, her love and care of him, his concerns for her and their child's welfare in past lives, all help to bring a certain comfort, though the contrast to the present keeps coming forcefully back. The poet's focus is very much on the woman—her despair, her feelings of abandonment, and her attempts to come to terms with the finality of her husband's departure.

Verses 103–117 take up the narrative. They relate the incidents associated with the Enlightenment, the Buddha's return to his father's kingdom to preach, the ordination of Rāhula, Yasodharā's decision to become a nun, her death, and the building of a *stūpa* in which her ashes are commemorated. All the incidents related are part of the familiar Buddha story. The Buddha's being present at her cremation and raining flowers on the bier is a poignant touch that comes from the *Yasodharāpadāna*.

The final two sections of the poem, verses 118–124 (which refer to events that occurred prior to her death but appear here after the event), and verses 125–130 (consisting of the homily), I consider later additions to the poem.

MODERN CRITICS OF THE *YASODHARĀVATA*

There has been a fair amount of criticism about the poem and Yasodharā's response to her husband's departure. On the one hand, traditional critics see her as the epitome of the good wife, who, even in the face of being abandoned by her husband, can still only wish him well. That is how the Buddha narrative presents her. Yet there are spaces within the narrative itself that provide possibilities for a more complex rendering of the character and reactions of Yasodharā.

As to be expected, early monks writing the Buddha narrative at first eliminate references to Yasodharā. The doctrinal concern is with the Buddha and his teachings. With time, she enters the story first as the nun and an *arahat*. Then later commentators and especially the folk poets fill in the lacunae elided in the earlier narratives with their own imaginings of her as the abandoned wife. Not only do they give a more complex and nuanced rendering of both the Bōdhisattva and Yasodharā but they present them in human, understandable terms.

Ediriweera Sarachchandra, a leading Sinhala critic, quotes verses 77, 78, 79, 82, 88, 98, and 100 of the *Yasodharāvata* (A) and states:

> In this set of verses queen Yasodharā does not lament about her own grief. She controls her sorrow and calls forth blessings on her husband. She asks how one who grew up amid the sheltered comforts of a royal palace can live in a forest. What can he eat? Can he sleep in comfort? Will he suffer from the heat of the sun? These verses reveal the genuine love of a village woman for her husband and child and a concern for their needs without a thought for herself. The reader's feelings are drawn to her for this reason.[34]

Sucharita Gamlath, another critic, asks: "What does Sarachchandra consider 'genuine love'? That a woman should not think of herself but of the needs of her husband and child? That she should sacrifice her entire life for them? Should her husband do the same for her? Sarachchandra and others maintain a curious silence on that question. For nearly half a century the 'Sarachchandra school' of critics have all interpreted these verses in this manner." Dr. Gamlath attributes such an interpretation to the patriarchal worldview that has pervaded Sri Lankan society. He claims, however, that the reader's sympathy for Yasodharā arises for a very different reason. It is because we are moved by pity for her fate as a victim

---

34. E. R. Sarachchandra, quoted in S. Gamlath and E. A. Wickramasighe, eds., *Yasodharāvata*. Colombo: Godage, 1995, pp. 65–67.

of a patriarchal society. "The desire to liberate her from the powerful grip of such a fate springs up in us."[35]

I think both critics (who represent two ends of a spectrum) fail to see the poem in its entirety. Dr. Sarachchandra excludes several verses in the lament where Yasodharā does sob and weep and mourn her loss. He ignores the fact that there is implicit blame in her repeated question, "Why did you leave without a word to me after all the years we spent together striving to attain your goal?" He excerpts only those verses that do permit the kind of interpretation he has chosen to make. Similarly, Dr. Gamlath, writing in a world and at a time more sensitive to a feminist viewpoint, sees Yasodharā merely as a victim. The power of the poem for him is a sense of pity for her fate.

The "folk" poet, however, has a more complex and more sensitive rendering of the situation. Verses 71–102 all deal with Yasodharā and her varying reactions to her husband's departure. The folk poet sees it neither as a one-dimensional uncritical acceptance on her part of her fate, which is how the Buddha story is narrated, nor as a pitiful victim of a patriarchal world, which is how Dr. Gamlath would have us see her, but as a very human woman faced with a terrible loss—a kind of death. However, like all human beings faced with the finality of a loss, she too tries to cope in the many ways women have—by recalling past happiness, mourning present absence, reproaching the lost love, questioning her own possible shortcomings. At the same time, because of her own great love, she wishes that no ill befall the loved one in this or any other existence. Having run through the gamut of emotions, the poet describes Yasodharā as achieving a degree of resignation. There is an acceptance of the reality of loss and an attempt to reconcile to it through the means provided by the culture—which in this context is one of Buddhist meditation and the striving to achieve *nirvāṇa*. This is what the 'work of mourning' helps to achieve and why rural women at funerals use this poem as a lament even today. The strength of the poem is in the range and complexity of emotions depicted, not just in a patriarchal or feminist reading of it.

The poem *Yasodharāvata* (A), though not considered part of the Sinhala literary canon, which consists of mostly classical works, is embedded in the popular imagination. Written in simple four-line stanzas with images that are neither new nor startling because they come from a popular repertoire, the poem nevertheless has a haunting cadence and an emotional power that has moved successive generations of readers and listeners by its very simplicity.

---

35. Sucharita Gamlath and E. A. Wickramasighe, eds., *Yasodharāvata*. Colombo: Godage, 1996, pp. 69–71.

CHAPTER ONE

The Poem

Yasodharāvata (The Story of Yasodharā) Also Known as *Yasodharā vilāpaya* (Yasodharā's Lament)

Through uncountable eons of measureless time[1] he perfected the
Virtues to become a Buddha.[2]
For yet more multiples of measureless time he perfected those same
Virtues
For still more eons multiplied uncountable times he strove to become
a Buddha.
Then as a bud matures and comes to bloom, he became a Buddha.

---

1. To indicate vast periods of *saṃsāric* time Buddhist cosmology deals in *asankya* (uncountables or immeasurables) and in *kalpa* (loosely translated as eons), all of which are ironically counted. The literal translation of the first line thus would be: "For four uncountables (*asankya*) times a hundred thousand eons (*kalpa*) he resolved to fulfil the Perfections." The second line refers to 'sixteen uncountables' and the next line to 'twenty-four uncountables'. It is as if by counting 'uncountables' one can make the concept of infinity imaginatively realizable. I have avoided the literal translation and tried to convey only the sense of vast periods of *saṃsāric* time, which is what the poet seeks to convey.

2. There are ten Perfections (*pāramita*) or virtues, that one must tirelessly cultivate throughout one's *saṃsāric* existences in order to become a Buddha. They are Generosity, Morality, Renunciation, Wisdom, Effort, Patience, Truthfulness, Resolution, Kindness, and Equanimity. The poet tries to indicate the enormity of that endeavor by the length of the time period involved. Here, I use the term Virtues (capitalized) instead of Perfections, which is how it is commonly translated.

2
Limitless the oceans of *saṃsāra* that he crossed
Boundless the wealth he gave away, even his eyes, flesh, head[3]
Tireless the single-minded efforts that he made
Countless the times he gave his life to be a Buddha.

3
Back in the days of the Buddha Dīpankara[4]
The Bōsat was born as the hermit Sumedha[5]
"That hermit by the marsh," proclaimed Dīpankara,
"Will one day in the future, be a Buddha."

4
The hermit made flower-offerings to Dīpankara,
Unwavering, single-minded, fully convinced.
He paid his respects with both hands flower-filled,
It was at Rambegam the prophecy was made.

5
From twenty-four Buddhas he received similar declarations.
He lived each life span to its full completion.
As Vessantara[6] he led a life of renunciation
His Acts of Generosity[7] then, were beyond comprehension.

6
The last of his many lives was spent in heaven,
He realized then he was very near his goal.
Gods enjoying bliss in the Brahma world,
Gathered in hundreds and thousands, to point the way.

---

3. This reference is to three specific Acts of Generosity related in the *Jātaka Tales*, a compendium of stories of the lives of the Bōdhisattva in his previous rebirths.

4. Buddhists believe that there were many Buddhas who lived and preached the Doctrine in different eons across *saṃsāric* time. Buddha Dīpankara preceded the present Buddha Gautama.

5. Sumedha, the ascetic, lay across a marshy rivulet so that the Buddha Dīpankara could walk over him and not muddy his feet.

6. Vessantara was known for his boundless generosity. He refused no request. He gave away his kingdom, wealth, and even his wife and children.

7. I use the phrase for the word *dāna*, which refers to meritorious acts of generous giving.

7
"Sir, the time has come for you to be a Buddha,
Give up this life of bliss. Set forth, my lord,
Think of past pieties performed and be reborn."[8]
It was for this the Bōsat[9] had waited so long.

8
He looked for the place where he was to be born, the land, the clan,
With patience sought who his parents were to be.
Who will I marry? What beauty is meant for me?
His All-seeing Eye saw Dambadiva[10] was the land.

9
Saw the womb of his mother, Māyā, wife of King Sudhōvan,[11]
Saw five hundred lovely women wet nurses,
Saw that his chief consort would be born at the same time.[12]
"I will now go to Dambadiva," he declared.

10
As Queen Māyā was sleeping on her golden bed,
All night long the full moon shone on her.
The gold-limbed queen then to her husband said,
"Through three watches of the night, my lord, the moon shone on my bed."

11
On a heavenly bed knee-deep in flowers
Sleeping alone, the queen saw in a dream
A precious gem drop deep into her womb.
"I do not know what is happening, my lord."

---

8. Buddhists believe that to become a Buddha one has to be born in the human world. Here the gods in heaven encourage the Bōdhisattva to return to earth and so complete his quest.

9. *Bōsat* is the Sinhala word for Bōdhisattva.

10. Jumbudvīpa or Dambadiva is the name for India in Buddhist texts.

11. This is the Sinhala form of Sudhōdhana.

12. Yasodharā in her many incarnations had been his chief consort.

12
As the Queen lay sleeping on her flower-strewn bed
She saw a silver rock from the sky descend.
A thousand queens stood guard around her bed.
She told the king about the dream she had.

13
"By the white sands of the Neranjanā river
I was bathed and my hair was washed,
Around me there arose a pleasing fragrance,
Dreams of childbirth followed one another.

14
"Hosts of maidens gathered flowers for me
In the Anotatta-lake[13] they made a bed for me.
A pair of virgin maidens then bathed me—
The Anotatta-lake appeared in a dream to me.

15
"A conch-white baby elephant stood before me
Who with his baby trunk caressed my belly.
Will some auspicious thing happen to me?
O handsome King, what do these strange dreams mean?"

16
That day the king invited holy Brahmins,
Fed them milk rice, and asked about the dream.
"That dream bodes ill to no one, O my king,
A Bōsat will be born to the world, O king.

17
"King Suddhōdana, since you ask, we say,
Bad dreams don't come to those who do good deeds.
A child will be born, that's what those dreams mean—
One of great Merit, over Three Worlds he'll hold sway."[14]

---

13. In Hindu Buddhist cosmology, this is a mythical lake at the foot of the mountain called Mēru at the center of the universe.

14. The three worlds in Buddhist cosmology are heaven or the formless world (*arūpa*), the human world or the world of form (*rūpa*) and the spirit world, hell, or the world of lust (*kāma*).

18
As the Queen was sleeping on her golden bed,
A golden garland lay upon her bed.
Gods slipped the golden garland over her head.
"This is what I dreamed at early dawn," she said.

19
"With parasols and flags a crowd surrounded me,
A golden star fell to earth beside me,
I picked it up quickly as if it were full of nectar,
Then deep into my womb sank that star."

20
As on her flower-filled bed Queen Māyā slept,
She dreamt she was seated on Mount Mēru's peak,
Saw a nearby village bathed in the full moon's beams.
"O king, what is the meaning of these dreams?"

21
As the queen slept on a bed made all of silver
Her dome-like breasts began to fill with milk.
A silver baby cobra coiled within her—
Such dreams of childbirth constantly assailed her.

22
Brahmins came to the palace vestibule
And explained in full the meaning of the dreams;
"A noble Bōdhisattva will be born, O Queen;
All Three Worlds he will rule, like the full moon."

23
Thousands of celestial maidens he left behind,
Abandoned a hundred thousand kinds of bliss,
Saw his noble mother Māyā, the infinitely good;
Then he descended from the sky, like a full moon.

24
Queen Māyā now has a pregnancy craving.[15]
Full of compassion, she gathers together the needy,

---

15. It is culturally accepted that a woman has special cravings during pregnancy. The nature of the cravings can indicate the personality of the fetus in the womb. In this case, they suggest a child of generosity and great compassion.

Commands that homes be built for all the poor,
And alms be also distributed there.

25
Queen Māyā has a second pregnancy craving.
The city gates now open and close continuously
As do the palace gates, opened for generous giving.
In this way Queen Māyā satisfies her craving.

26
Queen Māyā has yet another craving,
She wants the city to resemble one in heaven,
Orders a beautiful structure to be built,
Walks round the city and then enters it.

27
"I have a craving to take a walk in the *sāla*[16] grove."
The park is all decorated in silver and gold,
Four Guardian Gods come to keep careful watch,
They joyfully escort her round the grove.

28
The queen enters the *sāla* grove full of delight,
Flowers bloom, the sound of bees is all around.
The *sal* tree bends for the queen, lowers itself to the ground,
Aware the ten-month pregnancy[17] is complete.

29
The mother can now see the Prince within her—
A pure gold image enclosed in a jeweled case,
Decked in many wondrous ornaments;
At that moment all the gods appear.

30
She places her blessed hand on the trunk of the tree,
The flowering branch bends low as if to adorn her,
She grasps the lovely branch to ease her labor.
They draw rich and beautiful curtains around her.

---

16. The *sal* is a flowering tree famous in North India.

17. Pregnancies were believed to be ten or a little over ten month duration—perhaps calculated on a lunar calendar.

31
She had felt her pregnancy only after ten and a half months,
Her womb had hardly felt a cotton-wisp of weight.
The cool breath of flower-laden breezes wafted around;
In the *sāla* grove the baby prince was born.

32
Gods came through the sky and stood around her
Thousands of heavenly maidens surrounded her
The prince was born quickly, effortlessly.
Great Brahma held a golden net to receive the baby.

33
Like a moon the prince rests on the net of gold,
The lovely baby looks over the Three Worlds,
Aware there is none greater than he in all Three Worlds
The prince gives out a joyous lion roar.[18]

34
Seven lotus blossoms bloom for the baby Prince;
He stands on them and looks in four directions.
For Prince Siddharta who gave that noble roar
Gold-milk[19] is served to him without delay.

35
Wet nurses on either side surround him,
The ceaseless clamor of thousands is around him.
Then like a full moon shining very brightly,
He is taken to the palace with pomp and pageantry.

36
Thousands of guards are stationed to protect him,
Hundreds of thousands of heavenly flowers adorn him.

---

18. These events are all part of the Buddha story. The 'lion roar' he gives at birth indicates he will be a Supreme Buddha. He then takes seven steps on lotuses that magically appear.

19. It is a paste made of breast milk, a touch of gold, and other auspicious ingredients that is rubbed on a newborn's tongue for health, wealth, and rhetorical skills—a custom still performed in Sri Lanka.

Like a moon coming into fullness,
The Prince now comes into his sixteenth year.[20]

37
Our Bōsat acquires skills with bow and arrow
Yasodharā becomes his chief queen as before.
For twenty-nine years he lives the life of a layman,
Then gladly abandons all pleasures, leaves his queen.

38
Sick of *saṃsāra,* he turns to the ascetic path.
The king sends several queens to hold him back.
Disillusioned, he turns away from that pleasure-park.
"Whatever happens I will leave today."

39
The Bōsat rises quickly from his bed.
"I'll abandon pleasures, become an ascetic" he says.
"Who is that standing at the door?" he asks.
"It is I, Canna,[21]" lord, who's by your door."

40
"Virtues practiced over long years in *saṃsāra*
Are now complete, the heralded prince[22] has come.
I will become an ascetic when I've seen my son;
The fortunate Prince Rāhula has been born.

41
"My friend, our friendship stretches back through time.
Today will be my final royal journey.
Give me my rich and precious ornaments,
Prepare my horse, friend, deck him in his finery."

---

20. Sixteen years was considered the age of adulthood.

21. Canna was his minister and friend, throughout *saṃsāra*. The name is pronounced with a soft "ch" sound.

22. It was predicted that the day Siddharta's son was born he would leave the palace in his quest for Enlightenment. Now when he hears that his son is born he knows the time for his departure has come.

42
The minister weeps, tears stream down his face.
"I will now see my son and will come back," Siddharta says.
He goes to the royal palace where his wife resides,
And sees her in her bed, fast asleep.

43
He rests his blessed hand on the golden lintel
Places his blessed foot on the gold door-sill,
Sees her sleeping like a moon on her pure bed,
Withdraws his foot, turns away his head.

44
She sleeps on a bed heaped with lots of flowers
Milk flows from her swan-breasts for the baby prince
Yasodharā, full of Virtue, who has never done wrong,
Except perhaps, unwittingly, being a threat to Buddhahood.

45
Her hair falls loose, long, blue-black
Curls frame her face, like twirling tops.
The baby in her arms suckles content.
How can he leave once he's seen those golden breasts?

46
"From long ago I fulfilled all the Virtues
I practiced 'giving' to be a Buddha, to save all beings.
She is lovely, moon-like, preeminent among women —
Shall I just say one word to my dear queen?

47
"My lovely queen sleeps on her golden bed.
Shall I draw near, look at my baby by her side?
Her arm cradling him is a golden vine.
My eyes are drawn to my lovely, sleeping queen.

48
"The baby sucks his milk from that jeweled dome.[23]
What more is there to see, it is no use.

23. The Sinhala word is *mänik karandu* (jewelled relic casket). I use the word "dome" as a relic casket is dome-shaped like a *stūpa*. The English word "casket" has another shape and other connotations.

You have never failed me, not in thought or deed."
His mind holds firm, his eyes fill with tears.

49
"You've wept more tears for me than the seas hold water,
Does this wide world hold a woman as good as you?
Today I leave you in order to become a Buddha
I must destroy desire, be firm in my resolve.

50
"For one wife and one child shall I give up my quest?
Or save countless creatures from the *saṃsāric* round?
No, today I'll leave all I love, become an ascetic.
What a radiant lovely child is my Rāhula!

51
"By the power of our past resolves you and I are now prepared.
You are paramount among women, Bimbā[24] my queen.
No more will we walk together the *saṃsāric* round.
I will come back as a Buddha. Wait for me."

52
Sandalwood scent wafts over her flower-filled bed
That sweet fragrance for many leagues extends.
"Most beautiful are you, my Yasodharā,
I'll return when I become a Supreme Buddha.

53
"I leave my pure and gold-limbed queen behind,
I withdraw my foot without a backward glance.
I make this sacrifice to become a Buddha."
He steps back, walks away, a radiant sun.

54
"Canna, long have we two walked this path together.
We gave our word to each other, many lives ago"
The minister falls at the Bōsat's blessed feet
Asks, "Lord, where is it you now intend to go?

---

24. Bimbā was another name for Yasodharā.

55
"If you leave us our land will be deserted.
Don silken shawls, take a golden sword instead."
"Friend, do not impede my path to Buddhahood.
Deck out my horse and bring him to me now."

56
One does not argue with a Bōdhisattva.
Canna sobs, walks to the horse Kantaka.
Weeping hot tears he decks him in full finery,
Lifts his hand and strokes the animal gently.

57
The prince is dressed and now is ready to go
He presses his blessed feet on the threshold.
With his gold sword-tip he opens the golden door,
And thinks of his beloved son and of his Queen.

58
He leaves to become an ascetic to help all men.
She cuddles the sleeping child decked in ornaments.
Her blue-black hair hangs loose about the bed
Coils upwards and curls around her face.

59
On a bed strewn over with *saman* jasmine[25] flowers
The queen rests relaxed nestling her infant child.
Like a garland made of golden *kinihiri*[26] flowers
Her blessed arm cradles her baby child.

60
With his mind firmly set on becoming a Buddha
He forsakes past happiness for an ascetic life,
Forsakes the ties of love that bind to *saṃsāra,*
And those loose coils of blue-black, curling hair.

---

25. The flower is a Sri Lankan jasmine of great fragrance.

26. Spectacular golden flowers used in poetry as an image of softness and beauty.

61
Her gentle face that comforts with cool kisses
The lovely child held closely in her arms
Is like a golden star beside a full moon.
He leaves now, like the moon, thinking of his son.

62
Like the full moon the Bōsat steps outside.
"I go now to the forest, leave my gold-limbed child."
Gold-limbed he walks towards the river bank.
"I'll see my wife and child when I come back."

63
He's seen the ills of *saṃsāra* and is sickened.
He jumps astride his good horse Kantaka,
Crosses thirty leagues of woods and desert
Stops when he reaches the banks of the river.

64
Hooves beat down heavily, the horse leaps across the sand.
The animal opens his mouth and neighs aloud.
He flares his ears then turns his head around
And lovingly he licks the prince's feet.

65
It was the full moon night in the month of *Äsala.*[27]
He crossed the river, came to a sandy bank,
Took off his ornaments, gave them all to Canna,
Told him to re-cross the river and go back.

66
"How can I go back, my noble lord and master?
You leave us with an endless burning grief,
We are lost. Our sun has sunk behind the mountain.
How can I go back to that city, to wait for whom?"

---

27. *Äsala* is the eighth month (August) on a lunar calendar.

67
The Bōsat takes his gold sword in his hand
Cuts off his hair and throws it into the sky
Sahampati, god of heaven, takes the relic,
Makes the first offering of a monk's requisites.[28]

68
The weeping minister falls upon the earth.
The Bōsat lifts his hand to stroke his horse.
"Let us all three, break our bonds, go on to *nirvāṇa.*"
The weeping horse falls dead and is born in heaven.[29]

69
Grieving the loss of both the Bōsat and the horse,
"Do you send me home empty-handed?," Canna asks
"I must tell the king your father all that has happened.
Lord, give me leave to go, for that is now my task."

70
He gives him leave, and all his ornaments.
"Cross *saṃsāra*'s ocean waters, do not falter;
Tell the king my father to care for my young son;
Tell my queen Yasodharā to be comforted."

71
When the minister Canna returned to the city that day
The queen turned on him—a lioness leaping to the kill.
"Canna, friend, where is my lord, my beloved?
Go bring him to me now. I must see him, I will."

---

28. It is a tradition that when a monk first joins the Buddhist order, he is presented by a member of the laity with a set of eight basic requisites for a monastic life. They include two sets of robes, an undergarment, a begging bowl, a belt or carrying sash, a razor, needle and thread, and a cloth for filtering water. Here Sahampati, king of the Brahma heaven, makes the first ever such gift to the Bōdhisattva.

29. Heaven is a place where the gods live and to which those who do good go. But it is distinct from *nirvaṇa*.

72
Her combed hair falls like loosened strands of gold
Her full breasts like two domes made of pure gold.
Her lord gone to become a Buddha, to seek *nirvāṇa,*
Yasodharā falls on her bed and breaks into sobs.

73
"You left resolved, your mind set on being a Buddha.
I too made a firm resolve to be always your wife.
We made our joint resolves and you gave me your hand.
Why then did you leave today without a word?"

74
"We were first born in the animal world as deer,
Since that life we two have never been apart.
In every *saṃsāric* birth I was always your consort.
Why then in this life did you go, leaving me alone?

75
"Once we went as ascetics together to the forest,
We happily carried our two children in our arms,
We lived in two dwellings, separate, but in the same forest.
Why have you left me alone now, what have I done?

76
"With full awareness, I too made every effort.
By the power of our resolves we were always together,
With our joined hands we made all our gifts together.
Why then did you leave me, my lord, without one word?

77
"My eyes are full, my garments wet, tears fall,
As my husband, nectar-like, I recall.
Abandoning our son, I know he has now left.
Is there another woman in this world so bereft?

78
"Once in a former birth we were born as squirrels,
And our young one into the ocean's waters fell,
I know how hard you strove to save him then,
My husband, lord, why did you leave him now?

79
"Did I do wrong to bear you a handsome son?
Did I fall short in beauty, goodness, strength?
Was a disrespectful act unwittingly done?
Or did you dream of being a Buddha, conquering death?

80
"You must know, my lord, how the Kirala[30] hatches its eggs
Straining with its feet turned to the sky.
Flames of my grief rise up, they burn and scorch.
I beat my breast in grief and openly cry.

81
"In the shadows of the forests you now walk,
There is no resting-place for you in that dark.
Unceasing burns the fire that sears my heart,
O golden one, I beat my breast and weep.

82
"My moon-like lord who partook of fragrant food
That I, with special flavors, made for you,
May sweet fruits grow in the forest for you,
And fragrant flowers bloom for my lord of gold.

83
"Our flower-decked bed where we lay as our hearts desired,
I cannot look on it now—it burns my breast.
Striving to be a Buddha, unhindered, you went;
A searing sun now is the bed on which you slept.

84
"As Vessantara do you recall how you went to the forest?
Did I not look after you then, comb the forest for fruit?
A care never crossed your mind then, was that not the truth?
My moon-like-lord did I not constantly protect?

---

30. The *kirala* is the local name for a bird that has an unusual way of hatching its eggs.

85
"Like the marks on the moon was I not with you always?
Who told you then to abandon me today?
When I was asked to stay in Sandamaha city[31]
Did I not weeping, follow you that day?

86
"I did not protest when you gave away our children
Was I not then a Vessantara[32] that day?
Did I not bear you the lovely prince Rāhula?
Why then did you leave me and walk away?

87
"I never kept a secret from you ever,
I never let you be troubled, not me, Yasodharā,
I, once so blessed, now weep inconsolably,
Woman of a thousand virtues, I'm your Yasodharā.

88
"Your cause was Buddhahood—I sensed the signs
Yet I came with you as your wife, every time.
Now let meditation never leave my mind.
Ah! the palace is dark today, oh husband mine!

89
"You tied their hands and gave away our children
My golden breasts oozed milk for them, my young.
I fell at your feet and wept hot scorching tears.
To one who tried so hard, why do you cause such pain?

90
"Once both of us were born as *kindurās*[33]
We lived together on the dark moon rock.

---

31. The reference is to Yasodharā's decision to leave the palace and follow her husband Vessantara to the forest.

32. Vessantara is now synonymous with one who performs acts of incredible generosity. Yasodharā here claims the same title for herself in that she even let him give away her children.

33. Yasodharā in her grief recounts events in various past rebirths. Here the reference is to the *Kinduru Jātaka* when they were born as *kinduras*—mythical creatures, half human half bird—not unlike the mermaids in Western literature. A king out hunting saw them

Now beloved, in one night we are torn apart—
My heart is split. I can do nothing but sob.

91
"Countless times we gave away our children,
Countless tears I've wept because of you.
Tell me, have I ever wronged you, even unwittingly?
Why did you leave to become a monk, so secretly?

92
"In countless animal lives we perfected the Virtues
I have always been true to you, my love,
Why then do you do this to me now?
Am I not your Bimbā, your nectar-like Yasodharā?"

93
She tore off her precious pearl and gemstone jewels,
Took off her golden silks and the rings on her toes,
Pulled off the golden ornaments in her ears,
The queen sat lifeless as if turned to stone.

94
"I shall wait weeping and wailing, lamenting my woes,
Boundless tears will flow as I sob unceasingly,
Confused and troubled I now weep endlessly.
Why did you do this to me, depart as never before?

95
"When you were born as an elephant in the forest,
Did not a *vädda*[34] hurl his arrow and make you fall?
Did I not sit there beside you weeping and pleading?
O my husband why have you now abandoned our son?

---

and fell in love with the *kindura* woman. He killed the husband in an attempt to win her. She, however, refused to leave her dead husband. Hearing her laments and moved by her grief, the gods restored her husband to life.

34. *Vädda* is the term used to describe a group in Sri Lanka who were non-Buddhist and lived by hunting. They inhabited the forested areas of the island.

96
"When you were Mahausada[35] what didn't I do for you?
I rubbed a rice and curry paste on my head and limbs.
All those ordeals, however hard, were sweet to me
I was your Amarāvati then, now, your Yasodharā.

97
"I went with you on your countless ascetic journeys,
Joined in many forms of worship and offering.
I can't remember a wrong done even unthinkingly.
Why did you leave me so alone and solitary?

98
"My Lord, on a bed of forest flowers are you sleeping?
Your tender lovely feet are they now hurting?
Are there sufficient gods around you guarding?
Dear husband, my elephant king, where are you roaming?

99
"Whatever faults I may have had my lord,
I cooked and fed you flavored food and drink.
You who now wander far away in the forest,
May the blessings of the gods be with my lord.

100
"May all the forest fruits turn sweet for you.
May men surround you as do bees a flower.
May the sun dim his scorching rays for you.
May gods create shelters for you as you walk.

101
"My lord no longer hears my sad laments.
I don't see my gold-hued lord even in my dreams.
Now I too vow to renounce all worldly pleasures,
Though he has left me, I'll abide by the moral rules.[36]

---

35. The reference is to yet another *Jātaka* story of a previous birth of the Bōdhisattva. Yasodharā, then his wife Amaravati, rubbed a paste of rice and curry on her body so her imprisoned husband could lick it off and relieve his hunger when she visited him in prison.

36. These are the moral precepts that laymen undertake to perform in order to enter the path to *nirvāṇa*.

102
"My heavy grief I'll bear, however hard.
Like the air around me, I'll think only of my lord.
To become an *arahat* unswervingly I'll try
Till I set eyes on him again, I'll tell my rosary."[37]

* * *[38]

103
For seven days the Bōsat stayed in a mango grove,
On the seventh day, to Rajagaha he went.
With his All-seeing Eye saw what former Buddhas had done,
Then begged for alms, sat by the river and ate.

104
Leaving Rajagaha he said to King Bimbisāra,
"I'll preach a sermon to you when I return."
The Bōsat then went to the Ūruvela region,
Remained there as an ascetic for six years.

105
Having vanquished Māra, the fearful god of death,
He partook of milk-rice offered by Sujāta.
The noble one's face now waxed like a full moon.
He floated his golden bowl upstream on the river.[39]

106
Repeating a wish made far back in the beginning,
Sothiya the brahmin brought *kusa*[40] grass as offering,
The Bōsat happily accepted, walked to the Bōdhi tree[41]
Saw the twenty-one foot *Vajrāsana*[42] there.

---

37. Buddhists tell beads as in a rosary and recite the virtues of the Buddha. It is called the string of nine virtues.

38. The verses of lament end here and the Buddha narrative picks up again.

39. The bowl flowing against the current was a symbol that his Doctrine would be against the flow of normal desires.

40. It is a kind of grass that he can use to sit on.

41. The tree (*ficus religiosa*) under which the Buddha achieved Enlightenment.

42. The *Vajrāsana* is the immovable seat of Sakra. Here the Bōdhisattva sits on the seat under the ficus tree with the determination that he will not rise until he has achieved full Enlightenment. It thus becomes an 'immovable seat' or *vajrāsana*.

107
The Bōsat sat contemplating virtues perfected.
For his protection, the gods all gathered round.
Māra's hosts came too they filled the area around—
But he's now a Supreme Buddha, all bonds destroyed.[43]

108
To enable his Doctrine to last five thousand years
The Buddha, full of Merit looked over the earth.
To destroy all bonds, to save creatures from *saṃsāra*,
The Noble One preached the Sermon of the Turning Wheel.[44]

109
The noble Buddha looked with his All-seeing Eye
And made three visits, in consecutive order,[45]
Aware his life would last another forty-five years,
He went to his father's city to preach to him.

110
The gracious city was decked like a heavenly abode.
Five hundred *arahat*[46] monks accompanied him.
He gathered his kin, preached the Doctrine to them,
The city became enveloped in his halo of gold.

111
Like a tree of pure silver the weeping queen now comes,
The light of the Buddha's halo envelops her heart.
Like a lovely vine, escorted by her maidens, she comes,
Falls at the Buddha's feet and breaks into sobs.

---

43. The ten Impediments (*dasa bimbara*) such as lust, sloth, pride, and so on are a hindrance to a religious life.

44. The *dhamma cakka pavattana sutta* (verses that set the Wheel of the Doctrine in motion) was the first sermon that outlined the theory of causation basic to the Buddha's teachings.

45. The three visits are to the Tusita heaven to preach to his mother and the gods there, to the world of the nagas, and to his former home, Kapilavastu, to preach to his father and kinsmen.

46. *Arahats* have reached the final stage of the path to *nirvāṇa*.

112
Prince Rāhula asks his father for his inheritance,
Circling him, like a golden star around a moon.
The Buddha preaches the Doctrine, the prince is fully convinced,
Prince Rāhula is ordained and becomes a monk.

113
The Buddha preaches to the King, his father,
Eases his grief, sets him on the path to *nirvāṇa.*
Yasodharā gives up past comforts, becomes a nun,
With purity and wisdom keeps her vows.

114
She lived in this way, thereafter thought,
"I'll perform a miracle, rid men and gods of doubt."
The blessed queen pursued the life of a nun
Sat long hours in meditative trance.

115
All who do good, can earn the same rewards,
Discard Defilements,[47] quickly gain relief.
The queen now sits cross-legged, up in the air.
Says, "I'll get permission, follow the Discipline,

116
"And hereafter I'll be known as 'Rāhula Mātā.'"[48]
Soon the queen sheds all Impurities,
Then dies, and wins *nirvāṇa*'s highest bliss.
Five hundred maidens achieve bliss with her.

117
Her relics were enshrined in a beautiful *stūpa.*[49]
All paid their respects with a rain of flowers.

---

47. See note on Impurities.

48. Once she became a nun she was known not as Yasodharā but as 'Rāhula māta' (mother of Rāhula.)

49. A bubble shaped structure in which the ashes or other relics of the Buddha or arahats are preserved.

Siddharta, now a Buddha, rained Merit on her,
With his Buddha-hand placed flowers on her bier.

* * *[50]

118
She cast aside all worldly blessings and joined the order of the nuns.
She broke all earthly bonds of grief, as an *arahat*, brought glory to the nuns.
She made offerings to men and gods, when in the order of the nuns,
She obtained permission, attained *nirvāṇa*, the blessing that is beyond all blessings.

119
When the prophecy was made that in this eon he would be a Buddha,
You came with him like his shadow never left him anywhere.
From the time he became a Buddha, you lived apart, reached *nirvāṇa* first[51]
The many occult powers you gained, you exhibited everywhere.

120
Leaping over the seven oceans not permitting them to overflow,
You appeared in the ocean depths swimming like a fish below.
For the benefit of men and gods many miracles you did show,
Yasodharā of great fame, to *nirvāṇa* you did go.

121
Exhibiting various occult powers as offerings to the great *Muni,*[52]
Now rising up to the sky, in full sight of the great *Muni,*
Destroying grief, great Yasodharā reached the ultimate *nirvāṇa*
Can we not now recount your virtues together, in one voice?

---

50. I have marked a break to indicate a change in rhythm and style that occurs here. One of the palm leaf manuscripts conclude at verse 117. There is further internal evidence to support verse 117as being the conclusion of the poem. Yasodharā's death, and cremation are described in this verse. What follows refer to events that took place before her death and seem a later addition.

51. As related in the *apadāna*, Yasodharā dies and reaches *nirvāṇa* before the Buddha.

52. Another term used for the Buddha.

122
She sits in the three planes of the sky in their successive order.
She takes on the guise of Lord Sakra, great Brahma, the *Nāgas* and the *Garuda.*[53]
She tells the crowds that gather round "I am Yasodharā."
She sings the praises of Lord Buddha, on that day dies, attains *nirvāṇa.*

123
May all women bow your heads before the feet of Yasodharā.
Like a jeweled crown she adorns the heads of women everywhere.
Listen women, to this sermon decide to be born like her,
Plan to do every Act of Merit when this sermon you do hear.

* * *[54]

124
You creatures who wish to gain *nirvāṇa,*
See life's pain, shed your love of *saṃsāra,*
Grasp not wealth that can only bring sorrow,
Do Acts of Merit, do not in suffering wallow.

125
Women, take this sermon well to heart,
Angry looks on your husbands do not cast.
Like gold and mercury, live loving and united.
Be born like Yasodharā and be greatly blessed.

126
Think always of your husband's well-being,
Don't demand he bring you this or that.
Don't say a single word that might cause hurt.
Love him and live happily together.

---

53. The Garuda were mythical snake-eating birds. These are some of the miracles referred to in the *Yasodharāpadana.*

54. I have marked a break here because there is again a distinct break in rhythm and style. See introduction p. 27.

127
When things get rough and there is not much to spend,
Be kinder to him than when things were good.
It is not wrong, O women, to care for a husband.
Can't you too, like Yasodharā, reach *nirvāṇa*?

128
Like Yasodharā be always true to your husband.
Come ill or well be unchanging, faithful ever.
O women, if you love and are true to one husband.
You will surely enjoy future heavenly pleasure.

129
Be obedient to your husbands, all you women,
Do not be sad, and care for him when sick.
Be like Yasodharā who never thought of another.
Accumulate Merit so you can reach *nirvāṇa.*

130
All you women, fill your hearts with goodness.
Focus your mind constantly on good deeds.
Love all creatures, protect them from life's pain,
Then the nectar of *nirvāṇa* you will surely gain.

CHAPTER TWO

Comments on the *Yasodharāpadānaya*

The *Critical Pali Dictionary* defines the Pali term *apadāna*[1] as "tales in verse about the past karma of Buddhist Saints."[2] It has also been translated by scholars as sacred biographies of Buddhist saints or accounts of noble and heroic deeds, depending on the context in which it occurs. Some of the most well known are the Pali *apadāna* that give accounts of the lives of the Buddhist elders—monks and nuns. The *Yasodharāpadāna* is one of several such biographies contained in the Pali *apadāna*. It deals especially with the past lives of Yasodharā, wife of the Bōdhisattva and one of the earliest Buddhist nuns. Its intention, as with all the *apadāna* texts and much of the commentarial literature that developed around the early canonical texts, is didactic. Like the *Dhammapadaṭṭhakathā* or the *Jātaka Tales*, they belong to the genre of "homiletic literature" in which stories are used to illustrate and interpret doctrinal points, particularly for the edification of pious lay people."[3] The Sinhala term *apadānaya* has basically the same meaning and is used to describe the translations or 'transformations' of the Pali *apadāna* stanzas rendered in Sinhala prose around the thirteenth or fourteenth centuries C.E.

1. Note that the Sinhala term is *apadānaya* and the Pali term is *apadāna*. The meaning is the same.

2. *Critical Pali Dictionary*, vol. 1, p. 267. See also G. P. Malalasekera, *Dictionary of Pali Proper Names*, vol. 1, London: Pali Text Society, 1958, p. 115.

3. For a fuller analysis of the *apadāna* literature see Mellick, Sally, "The Pali Apadāna Collection." *Journal of the Pali Text Society*, XX (1994), 1–42.

The *Yasodharāpadānaya* is a Sinhala work based on the Pali *Yasodharāpadāna* stanzas. It is a considerably expanded prose version of that text and while it includes stanzas in Pali from the *Yasodharāpadāna*, the explanation in Sinhala that follows is often much more than a translation.

I had not intended to translate in full the Sinhala *Yasodharāpadānaya.* I came upon the text when I was looking at manuscripts of the *Yasodharāvata* in the National Museum Library in Colombo. I realized when reading those manuscripts that the *Yasodharāpadānaya* was clearly the source for the added section to the text I was translating and therefore of considerable interest. I then decided to translate the full text, even though certain sections seem repetitive and suggest possible later additions or errors in the process of transcribing. I have italicized those sections in my translation.

Since it was the practice in monasteries for a senior monk to read a text out aloud while a group of other monks wrote it down, errors could and did often occur. This also happened when monks recopied manuscripts.[4] Constant transcribing was, however, the only method both for preserving and ensuring the continued existence of multiple copies of venerated texts for posterity. The practice was therefore a constant activity in monasteries from very ancient times and continued into the early twentieth century.

My translation is of the text *Yasodharāpadānaya* edited by the late Dr. Meegoda Pannaloka Thēra and published by the Sadeepa Book Shop in Colombo in 2000. In his introduction, Dr. Pannaloka Thēra states that it was based on a palm leaf manuscript No. B 5 at the Library of the Dhammagaveshana Association. He adds, "It became clear to me as I was editing this text that in ancient Sri Lanka there were several prose and verse versions of the *Yasodharāpadānaya.* What is most widespread among us is the *Yasodharāpadānaya* in Pali verse that is included in the *Thēri Apadāna* of the *Khuddaka Nikāya.*[5] Apart from this there is the *Yasodharāpadānaya* that appears with slight variations in the Pali text edited by the Senior Monk Polvatte Buddhadatta. He has also drawn attention in a footnote to a set of verses belonging to another text of the *Yasodharāpadānaya* that are included in this text. He says, "It was clear in editing the *Yasodharāpadānaya* that the verses that appear from time to time in the text come from the Pali

4. The practice is also referred to in Meegoda Pannaloka Thēra's text.

5. There is the suggestion here that the Sinhala texts were prior to their formulation in the Pali *apadāna*, but though this is true of other commentarial texts such as the *Dhammapadaṭṭhakathā*, there is nothing in this text or colophons in the Pali versions to confirm that.

Yasodharāpadāna as well as from other less well known manuscripts. Some verses clearly come from the *Buddha Vamsatthakatha*."[6]

The Pali *Yasodharāpadāna* is considered a first or second century CE text. Even if it had not been based on an earlier Sinhala version, it would still be one of the earliest commentarial texts that deal with Yasodharā, the wife of the Bōdhisattva. It is natural that this early reference to her is in her role as a nun. Such an expansion of her persona would be a fitting subject for a monk. While a few details from the text have filtered into popular lore, the *Yasodharāpadāna* is known mainly to monks and scholars. In this it is very unlike other twelfth and thirteenth century CE texts that became popular with lay Buddhists such as the *Pūjāvaliya* (Garland of Devotion), the *Butsaraṇa* (Refuge in the Buddha), or the *Amāvatura* (Nectar-like waters [of the Doctrine]).

The character of Yasodharā as she appears in the *apadāna* is of a strong and confident nun. It is she who decides on the timing of her own death and on preceding the Buddha to *nirvāṇa* so that the people do not have to "face a double loss" if she and the Buddha die at the same time (as they were destined to do). Again, in performing the ritual ceremony of farewell common to all monks and *arahats*, she does so with great confidence and poise. She is no more the grieving wife, but now an *arahat* in her own right and confident of her powers. She comes "to apprise" or "to announce" to the Buddha her decision and impending departure. The Sinhala word is *säla karati*. It is stronger than the word "to tell."

> "Auspicious Lord who has shared with the world and with me the taste of *nirvāṇa*, there are some words I would respectfully like to say to you. Listen then."

She goes on

> "I wish to apprise you O great Teacher that I am now seventy-eight years old. I have reached the steep precipice [that leads] to death.

The Buddha in turn acknowledges "how great a help she had been and her infinite goodness" and goes on to praise her intellectual achievements and the supernormal powers she has acquired through her life of meditation. At his request she performs miracles for the public of monks and laity. In one of those appearances she takes on the form of a Maha Brahma "with a thousand lightning flares

6. Meegoda Pannaloka Thēra, ed., *Yasodharāpadānaya*. Colombo: Sadeepa, 2000, p. 3. The translation is mine.

emanating from her ten fingers lighting up ten thousand universes." Having completed the display before the whole world and the Brahmas, she turns to them and says with great dignity emphasizing her human condition, "I am not a god or a Brahma. I am but a noble woman who in *saṃsāra* was the devoted companion of Gautama Buddha." Thereafter she proceeds to give an account of her many acts of devotion to the Bōdhisattva during their long journey in *saṃsāra*.

The Sinhala *Yasodharāpadānaya* expands and elaborates the account of the miracles Yasodharā performs, thereby giving her an aura of divinity and establishing her as a powerful *arahat* of supernormal powers. However, this is tempered by her own account of her many human acts of devotion to the Bōdhisattva performed in their journey through *saṃsāra*. The fact that such acts are not merely described but that in the text Yasodharā recounts them all herself, many of them poignant human accounts of sacrifice and generosity on her part because of her great love for the Bōdhisattva, make it a very human and personal recitation. The second section of the text is her recapitulation of what the Buddha said about her when he proclaimed her virtues to his father, King Suddhōdhana. It is a more formal recitation where the repetition is mainly for its incremental effect and may have been added later to emphasize the point. The intention of the text *Yasodharāpadānaya* is to create a portrait of the nun Yasodharā as a woman of great Merit and character, a powerful, almost divine being, and an example and role model to laypersons.

CHAPTER THREE

The Prose Text

Yasodharāpadānaya
(The Sacred Biography of Yasodharā)

I salute the Blessed One, the Worthy One, the Enlightened One.[1]

Our Lord Buddha, the most auspicious and brightest ornament[2] of the Sakya clan, Teacher of the Three Worlds, in the forty-third year of his Enlightenment, traversed in succession the towns and villages of the kingdom. He went from the city of Sävät to the city of Rajagaha, from there to a beautiful and pleasing cave on the Gijakūta mountain, and resided there.

At that time the Thēri (Senior nun) Yasodharā, accompanied by thousands of *bhikkhunis* (nuns), left her nunnery, went to see the Buddha, worshipped him, sat respectfully on a side, listened to a sermon, and at its conclusion took her leave and returned to her nunnery. The next evening, sitting in the half lotus position she attained a Trance State and thought thus, "The Lord Buddha's final release into *nirvāṇa*[3] and my release from life are to take place on the same day. If that were to happen people in this world will be faced simultaneously with a

1. From the palm leaf manuscript B/5 in the library of the Dharmagaveshana library, edited by the monk Meegoda Pannaloka Thēra (Colombo: Sadeepa, 2000).

2. The Sinhala word is *tilaka*, which means the mark on the forehead signifying both a sign of auspiciousness and a position of eminence. I have taken the liberty to translate the meaning rather than the word.

3. Literally means to extinguish. It is the final goal of Enlightenment.

double loss and will not be able to bear it. Therefore it is better that I should go to the state of *nirvāṇa* before him." Knowing that two years hence the Buddha would attain *nirvāṇa* she thought, "I will therefore go immediately, make my farewells, get forgiveness and this very night reach *nirvāṇa*." At that moment strange miracles occurred. Then she went to the nunneries of eighteen thousand nuns who had performed Acts of Merit and faithfully served the Buddha and her[4] over an infinite period in *saṃsāra*. They all [went to the Buddha] worshipped him and lovely as a galaxy of stars shining around a moon, applauding "sadhu" (good! good!) informed him that she had come.

"Auspicious Lord, who has shared with the world and me the taste of *nirvāṇa*, there are some words I would respectfully like to say to you. Listen then," she said.

> *Atthasattati vassāmhi pavajīmo va tatthivayo*
> *Pabhārahi anuppattā ārocemi mahā muṇī*[5]
>
> [I wish to apprise you, O great teacher that I am now seventy-eight years old. I have arrived at the steep slope of death.][6]

"Moreover, Buddha, Lord, I have now completed seventy-eight years. I am thus in my declining decade. Though that be so, as all *arahats* (enlightened noble ones) on the day they are to attain *nirvāṇa*, come to the Buddha, bid farewell and obtain forgiveness, and as it is a tradition performed over generations, now I too Lord wish to do the same," she said.

---

4. The Sinhala text reads "*buduntada matada*—to the Buddha and to me" which suggests that it is still part of Yasodharā's speech. If so, the tense would have to change.

5. Often in Sinhala Buddhist texts a Pali verse is first given in Pali and the Sinhala paraphrase or expanded explanation follows. The Pali verses in this Sinhala text are sometimes identical to the PTS version and sometimes different. I have decided to give the translation of the Pali as it appears in the Sinhala as they are not always identical to the Pali.Text Society edition of the *Yasodharāpadāna* by M. E. Lilley and translated by Sally Mellick Cutler into English. This verse, however, happens to be identical to verse No. 9 of the PTS edition. Dr. Meegoda Pannaloka Thēra identifies most of the verses included in the Sinhala *Yasodharāpadānaya* as coming from a text titled *Yasodharāpadāna Gātha* edited by Polvatte Buddhadatta Thēra (from extant palm leaf manuscripts) and published in 1930. This verse is identified as verse 950 in that text.

6. I give the English translation of the Pali verses in the text even though the Sinhala text explains and expands on the Pali in the body of the text itself. The general Buddhist public knew little Pali and so the verses had to be explained.

Saṃsaritvāca saṃsāre khalitaṃ ce mamaṃ tayiṃ
ārocemi mahāvīra aparādam khamessu me.[7]

[Great Hero I apprise you. When I was traveling through *saṃsāra*, if I have done you any wrong, forgive me.]

Thus when the Thēri Yasodharā asked permission of the Buddha and recounted the details of her past lives in *saṃsāra*, at her words the Lord looked out over the past in *saṃsāra* and saw the following.[8] How so? Knowing how great a help she had been and her infinite goodness during their past in *saṃsāra* he said, "There is no woman comparable to Yasodharā in this entire Buddha era. This revered person is one who has the knowledge to see uncountable eons of past lives. She has acquired the Divine Eye and Divine Ears[9] and has the unique and special powers of sight and hearing. She has extinguished all Defilements.[10] She has arrived at the summit of the Three Kinds of Knowledge. She has supernormal powers not second to the Buddha. From the day she became an *arahat* she has continued to live as an ordinary nun and did not exhibit her miraculous powers. Thus none have seen the power of her miracles. Men living in the world do not know what kind of a person the Mother of Rāhula is. Is she an *arahat* or is she not? Does she have miraculous powers or does she not? They have doubts. Therefore Thēri Yasodharā, it is not right that one of such great Merit as you should disappear privately into the state of *nirvāṇa* without displaying your powers to the world. You should perform some miraculous acts," he said.

At this, she thought, "having obeyed him in numerous past lives now in this last life I should do likewise, and in accordance with the wishes of the Buddha I will display my supernormal powers and perform miracles."

She then turned to the Buddha, worshipped him and said, "You O Buddha of heroic strength, who successfully accomplished in four *asankya* (uncountables) times a hundred thousand *kalpa* (eons) what other bōdhisattvas took sixteen *asankya* times a hundred thousand *kalpa*, or eight *asankya* times a hundred thousand *kalpa* to accomplish. I, who am now displaying miraculous powers before a

---

7. This is verse 14 of the *Pali Apadāna*. which I will call PA, and verse 965 of the *Yasodharāpadāna Gatha*, which I will hereafter call YG. The verses are again almost identical.

8. The Sinhala text reads "*esē du vu sēka*"—that was so." Perhaps an error for "*esē dutu sēka—saw as follows.*"

9. These are special powers of sight and hearing that noble beings who have reached the final stage in the path to Enlightenment acquire.

10. The Sinhala term is *keles.* Pali *klesha* is a Buddhist concept translated as Defilements or Impurities.

Supreme Buddha such as you, I am Queen Yasodharā, who was your chief queen, the head of all your ninety-six thousand queens when you were Siddharta in the past.

"Moreover following the teachings of my Lord I will [soon] realize the great deathless state of *nirvāṇa*. I will come ashore from the sea of *saṃsāra*. In order that I should not be born again in *saṃsāra* I have dug out the root of desire with the sharp point of *kagiyāsi*[11] [meditation on the components of the impermanent body].

"In order that I never become a wife to any other man, you have given me the mirror of the *tilakunu* [three characteristics of Impermanence, Suffering, and Soullessness].

"So that I do not bear another child you have given me the contraceptive of the *tilakunu* that has the components of love and friendship. So that I do not have to wear the dirt of shawls and ornaments, you gave me the ornament of the *tacapanca kastāna* [the sword of the Five Elements of Impermanence],

"To counter the poison of the sweets one eats over innumerable lives you gave me the antidote of the *dasa pilikul pas vikum* [Five Victories over the Ten Revulsions," she said.

"Thus Lord, you gave me, who was wandering in the dark of Ignorance, the lamp of the Divine Eye to see my past lives over incalculable eons and light the way to the state of *nirvāṇa*.

"Therefore O Lord Buddha by the supernormal powers given by you, behold now one such miracle." So saying she gave a lion roar, worshipped the blessed feet of the Buddha, obtained permission, attained to a Trance State, rose up into the sky and said,

yasodharā ahaṃ vīra arahati pajāpati
sākiyamahī kule jātā itthīyāge patitthitā[12]

---

11. These are concepts from Buddhist Doctrine. I have kept the Pali term as the writer does, and explained it in parentheses.

12. Verse 18 of the PA; verse 965 of YG. Again, the verses are almost identical.

> [I am Yasodharā, O Hero, a woman, born to the Sākyan clan, and your wife during your lay life.]

Then she cried out aloud for the gods living in tens of thousands of universes to hear.

> *Cakkavāla samaṃ kāyaṃ sīsaṃ uttarane kuruṃ*
> *ubhopakkhedeva dīpe jambudīpaṃ sharīram kaṃ*[13]

> [a body like the sakvala world system; a head like the northern continent of Kuru, two wings like the eastern and western continents, the full body like Jambudipa.]

She thought, "I will make an offering to the Buddha from the abode of the Garudas." She took on the guise of a Garuda which had a neck the size of the Mēru rock, two eyes as big as moons, a right wing as large as the continent on the East (*purvavideha*), a beak as big as the rock of the universe (*sakvala*) and a Garuda body so large as to cover the entire universe so that it looked as if wrapped with a canopy on which the universe was painted without leaving even a sliver of space.[14] Then she tore up from its root the enormous (*damba*)[15] tree, a hundred leagues tall. Waving it like a fan over the Buddha and conveying a sense of momentary ease to the Buddha's body, she made the offering of the 'seven Garuda abodes' and cried out aloud "I am the Thēri Yasodharā."

> *Hasti vaṇṇaṃ tathe vassaṃ sabbataṃ jaladhi tathā*
> *Candimaṃ sūriyaṃ meruṃ vasakka vaṇṇañca dassayī*[16]

> [She then displayed herself in various forms; as an elephant, a horse, a mountain and an ocean, then as the sun, moon, Mount Mēru and Sakra.]

Thus of ten such miraculous displays she created an elephant image covering the sky for ten thousand leagues. Then she stretched out her hand to the city of

---

13. Verse 24 of the PA; verse 971 of YG.

14. Note the much elaborated explanation of the Pali stanza in the Sinhala text.

15. The Sinhala reference is to a *damba* tree—a common forest tree—but the Pali stanza here refers to a *jambu* tree which was more familiar in India and from which the land took its name as *jambudīpa*.

16. Verse 27 of the PA is almost identical. The explanation in the text, however, is much elaborated.

Sakra, tore out the divine *Madara* tree and made a royal umbrella of flowers to hold over the Buddha's head. While the crowds in unison applauded shouting "Sadhu" (good, well done) she cried out loud, "I am none other than Yasodharā who was the Buddha's wife when he lived the life of a householder."

> *Brahma vaṇṇañca māpetvā dhammaṃ desesi suññataṃ*
> *Yasodharā ahaṃ vīra pādevandāmi cakkhuma*[17]
>
> [Then having taken the form of god Brahma she preached about emptiness. I am Yasodharā, O Hero. I pay homage at your feet, Clear Sighted One.]

Then, creating a twelve league tall figure of Mahā Brahma with a thousand lightning flares emanating from the ten fingers of two hands lighting up ten thousand[18] universes, and sitting cross-legged up in the sky for the whole world to see, she superceded eleven hundred and fifty *lakhs*[19] and twenty thousand Brahma kings. She then said to them, "I am not a god or Brahma. I am but a noble woman who in *saṃsāra* was the devoted companion of Gautama Buddha." Thereafter the Thēri Yasodharā sat in the sky and like one who takes a single fistful of gold water and produces different ornaments she performed miracles, and as it could not be recounted fully even by the Buddha she preached a sermon in the manner of a Buddha. Then miraculously descending and descending into the midst of gods, Brahmas, men and noble disciples, like the seven gems falling from the sky onto a universal monarch, she worshipped the Buddha with her hands upraised and said, "O Gautama, Lord Buddha, if there are any shortcomings in the miracles I displayed or the sermon I preached do forgive me. Moreover, look on it with the lamp of *saṃsāra*.

"I have been faithful to you my lord through all of *saṃsāra* and this is now my final appearance. Because of the acts of devotion I performed to a Buddha like you throughout *saṃsāra* and because you and I swam across the sea of Defilements in the ship of Faith and escaped ashore from the deeps of *saṃsāra* I will now relate the acts of devotion I have performed.

---

17. Stanza 28 of the PA; verse 976 of YG.

18. The Sinhala text reads *dasahasak*, either a mistake for *dahasak—thousand* or probably a variant or corruption of *dasa sahasak—ten thousand*. I have translated it as the latter.

19. A *lakh* is 100,000. As often happens, the numbers, though conveying a sense of specificity, are intended just to suggest enormity.

"Right here, looking at *saṃsāra* by the power of the Divine Eye that can see uncountable past lives and which I acquired as a result of the offerings of oil and lights I made in life after past life, I see that uncountable are the number of lives in which I sacrificed my life to save yours, my Lord.

Neka kōti[20] *sahassāni bhojanatthā yadāsi maṃ*
Natatha vimanā homi tuyhatthāya mahāmunī[21]

[In uncountable millions of past existences you gave me away for food
Yet I was not distressed. It was for your benefit Great Sage.][22]

"O Buddha Lord of the World when you were perfecting Virtues in this great *saṃsāra* and were endowed with great riches and ruled as King Vessantara I was your chief queen. Then when supplicants came to you and begged, 'Great King give us your chief queen,' you looked at my face and saw I was not upset. This happened in uncountable numbers of lives, I know.[23]

Neka kōti sahassāni bhojananthā yadāsi maṃ
Natatha vimanā homi tuyhatthāya mahāmunī

[Lord of the World, in uncountable millions of past existences, when you and I lived together in *saṃsāra* I know you sold me for food [to survive.]

Neka kōti sahassāni jīvitāni pariccajiṃ
Bhaya mokkạ karissanti vajāmi mama jīvitaṃ[24]

[In uncountable millions of past existences I gave my life for you.
Yet I was not afraid. It was for you I gave my life.]

"Moreover, Buddha, Lord, who spent your days in this *saṃsāra* that has no beginning or end, because of your high ideals, I know uncountable are the

---

20. *Kōti*—10,000,000.

21. This is stanza 38 of the PA; verse 983 of YG. This and the following verse are identical. The first of the two is possibly an error in transcribing as the explanation that follows is not related to the verse.

22. Note that the explanations that follow do not necessarily always relate to the text of the Pali stanza. They sometimes digress widely.

23. This phrase is repeated again and again at the end of each verse, giving the stanzas a kind of patterning.

24. Verse 39 in the PA; verse 986 in YG.

number of lives in which you gave me away as a gift and as a help to debtors and merchants. Yet I was not distressed by it.

Neka kōti sahassāni siṃha viyāgaghādī vadanam gugaguru
Tuyeha gandanī sammuhatta mimmāyi[25]

[In uncountable millions of past existences while you and I travelled *saṃsāra* together, when lions, wolves, crocodiles and bears came roaring to eat you I gave my life to them to save you.]

"Lord Buddha, you who are unafraid of Mara, when you and I traveled together through numerous lives in *saṃsāra*, when lions, tigers, crocodiles, bears, devils, and demons ran roaring towards you, I who stood behind, pushed past you and faced them and not thinking about my own life, threw myself into their jaws and saved you, in uncountable numbers of lives, I know.

Then saying, "How can I allow women to sacrifice their lives to protect a man like me," you too sacrificed yourself, in uncountable numbers of lives, I know.

"Lord Buddha, you who without fearing *saṃsāra*, plunged into the sea of Perfections,[26] when devils and demons captured you in this *saṃsāra* and subjected you to various forms of torture, I gave my life as hostage and saved you from such dangers during uncountable numbers of lives, I know.

"Besides Lord Buddha, you who because of your compassion for all creatures [allowed yourself to] become mired in the Defilements of *saṃsāra*, and when because of the evils of *saṃsāra* you suffered different forms of torture and imprisonment, you mortgaged me and escaped from those kinds of suffering, in uncountable numbers of lives, I know.[27]

[*There you mortgaged me and escaped from those kinds of suffering and thereafter I saved myself from suffering in uncountable numbers of lives I know.*[28]]

---

25. There is no corresponding stanza in the PA. However, the Pali verse that is interpolated is then explained and expanded in the Sinhala text that follows.

26. The reference is to the Bōdhisattva's conscious decision to fulfill the ten Perfections or Virtues needed to be a Buddha, and which have to be achieved while in *saṃsāra*. See glossary.

27. The repeated stanza has the word *mama* (*I myself*), which did not appear in the earlier stanza but does make the sense clearer.

28. I have italicized what seems an exact repetition with a single word different.

"Moreover, Lord Buddha, you who confounded Mara, uncountable are the times in which I persuaded executioners who take pleasure in this troubled *saṃsāra,* to save me, and by my own powers I rescued myself from disasters and achieved happiness, in uncountable numbers of lives, I know.

"Lord Buddha, when trapped in the bonds of Mara in this *saṃsāra,* you abandoned me and sought other women and [as a result] were subjected to various forms of torture and imprisonment. I, when I learned of it, without the slightest trace of anger, like a mother, heart stricken by the suffering of a son, with a loud cry rushed there, gave them my silks and jewels as payment and saved you lord, in uncountable numbers of lives, I know.

"Moreover, as I had resolved throughout *saṃsāra,* to devote myself only to you, I donated all my goods, wealth and ornaments to them on your behalf, in uncountable numbers of lives, I know.

"Again, I know, uncountable are the lives in *saṃsāra* when abandoning enormous wealth, renouncing family and kinsmen, without telling anyone, secretly I ran away with you and worked as a menial servant to support you. You in turn performed hard labor to support me, in uncountable numbers of lives, I know.

"You, Lord Buddha, when traversing *saṃsāra,* gave away whole villages filled with followers, cattle and buffaloes, in uncountable numbers of lives, I know.

"Again, while dwelling in *saṃsāra* you donated storehouses filled with grain in uncountable numbers of lives, I know. Besides, you abandoned homes filled with every luxury, providing every comfort, chewed and spat out like a ball of spittle, in uncountable numbers of lives, I know.

"Moreover, you donated auspicious royal elephants and chariots in uncountable numbers of lives, I know. You who stood firm against Māra, yet tied their hands and gave to supplicants the children I bore from my womb when we lived in *saṃsāra.* [This happened] in uncountable numbers of lives, I know.

"When you lived with me in *saṃsāra,* because you were attached to the idea of giving you gave away our children. When I bore you yet more children, you gave them too away to supplicants. Yet I was not distressed. [This happened] in uncountable numbers of lives, I know.

Furthermore when we were living in *saṃsāra,* you gave away all your wealth to supplicants and because you were attached to [the idea of] giving, you gave them [even] the clothes and ornaments on my hands and neck, in uncountable numbers of lives, I know.

> [*Moreover, abandoning enormous wealth in saṃsāra, renouncing family and kinsmen, without telling anyone, secretly, I ran away with you and worked as a menial servant to support you. You in turn performed hard labor and supported me in uncountable numbers of lives I know.*
>
> *You Lord Buddha, when traversing saṃsāra gave away whole villages filled with followers, cattle and buffaloes in uncountable numbers of lives I know.*
>
> *Again while dwelling in saṃsāra you donated storehouses filled with grain in uncountable numbers of lives I know. Besides, you abandoned homes filled with every luxury, providing every comfort, chewed and spat out like a ball of spittle.*][29]

"When you took off your ornaments and regalia and gave them away I was not distressed. It happened in uncountable numbers of lives, I know.

"Moreover, you Lord Buddha who know *saṃsāra* having crossed it, when you gave up the kingdom of Sakra and the pleasures of Brahma and took to the forest as an ascetic, I, who at the time was living in the palace amidst great wealth and luxury, while going from the upper story to the lower story [saw you and] was distressed. I who was your chief queen, who had been brought up in such luxury, shed all desire for such comforts as if shedding something unclean[30] and went with you. And when we lived together as ascetics, while you remained in the leafy hermitage I carried baskets full of forest fruits and roots for you, in uncountable numbers of lives, I know."

In this manner she worshipped the Buddha and declared all her acts of devotion and the Perfections she had cultivated. At that time gods and Brahmas wished to know what Acts of Merit this Queen Yasodharā had done in the past to be able to perform such miracles and obtain such wonderful powers.

Then the Lord who knew the minds of others, realized the wishes of the vast gathered crowds and consoled Yasodharā saying, "*Thēri* Yasodharā, tell the

---

29. This seems again to be an exact repetition of three earlier verses. It may have been a scribal error in the original manuscript or a printer's error at publication. I have put the passage in italics.

30. There is an alternative in a manuscript that reads *apavithrayak—something unclean*, though this text reads *apavisthrayak*.

crowd gathered here of your initial determined commitment which was the cause of your devotion to the Buddha and you yourself rid the crowds gathered here of their doubts."

When she heard this from the Buddha she thought, "It seems as if my Lord wishes me to give an account of my initial determined commitment myself." She worshipped the Buddha, looked at the great crowd gathered there and said, "Look you creatures, do you think I am a woman who has done but a little Merit? Do not think so. There is no other woman in this Buddha era as blessed and as fortunate as I. I shall tell you the reason for this. Listen then. The eighty distinguished monks of the Buddha fulfilled the Perfections for one hundred thousand *kalpa* (eons). The [two] chief disciples fulfilled the Perfections for one *asankya* (uncountable) plus one hundred thousand *kalpa.* Not so with me. How so? From the distant past throughout four *asankya* (uncountables) and one hundred thousand *kalpa* I have constantly accompanied my Lord and without fail fulfilled the Perfections with him.

"Meritorious ones, I have provided great feasts of food and water to the supreme Buddhas such as the Buddha named Brahmadēva, of determined mind, the Buddha Gautama, firmly fixed in his words, and the Buddha Dīpankara. [I did so] in order to obtain firm predictions [*varam*][31] from them. Listen then to what I say.

"When I lived in *saṃsāra* with my Buddha, the great earth 240,000 [leagues] thick, was not sufficient to contain the alms for monks which I prepared and offered.

"The waters of the ocean, 84,000 leagues deep, would not be sufficient for dissolving the salt I used for the gruel I prepared. So it was with the salt, water, molasses, oil, and lemon that I used. Therefore ye gods and men, know that it was no small Act of Merit that I performed.

"Further when my Buddha saw some other Buddha and performed some Act of Merit for him, I participated with him in those Acts of Merit without fail, and I made an independent fervent wish.

31. The word is almost untranslatable. It is a guarantee or warrant given by a Buddha or deity that such a thing that one has wished and worked for will come to pass.

"For that reason, in order to convey the amount of alms I myself had given and the number of Feasts of Giving I myself had performed, this was the sermon given by our Buddha before the king his father, at Kapilavastu.

"When I wept, clutching the feet of my lord Buddha, the Supreme One, Teacher of the Three Worlds, the Buddha who could in one instant with his Divine Eye see into the hearts of creatures said:

> "*Sāro maṇḍā varo ceva maṇda kappe jiṇo duve*
> *Aññasamiṃ asaṃkheyyā pañca kappā vibhāvitā*
>
> [The eon when one Buddha appears is the Sara kalpa; when two are born it is the madda kalpa. It is not possible to count the rest of the eons because only five are known.]
>
> *Eko buddho sāra kappe maṇdakappe jiṇā duve*
> *Vara kappatayo Buddhā cathuro sāra maṇdake*
> *Pañcha buddhā bhadda kappe tatho natvadhikā jiṇā*[32]

"The eon when a single Buddha is born is termed a *sārakalpa*. When two Buddhas are born that age is called the *maddhakalpa*.[33] The age when three Buddhas are born is called the *varakalpa*. The eon when four Buddha's are born is called the *sāramaddhakalpa*. The age when five are born is called the *bhadrakalpa*. Hear it then from me.[34]

"This Queen Yasodharā herself, full of faith, offered alms to all the Enlightened Ones who became Buddhas in all these *kalpa* (eons). Listen then Great king and keep well in mind the Acts of Giving she has performed," said the Buddha.

---

32. These verses are not from the PA. Pannaloka Thera identifies them as from the *Buddhavamsa commentary.* The explanation that follows the verses is here a close rendering of the Pali and so I have not given a separate translation of it.

33. The Pali word is *mandakappa*, but the Sinhala word is consciously kept as *maddhakalpa.*

34. Here the explanation accurately follows the Pali text. At this point it is the Buddha who is making a statement about Yasodharā.

"*Pañca kōti sata Buddhā navakōti satā nica*
ētesaṃ deva devānaṃ mahā dānaṃ pavattayiṃ[35]

[Listen O great king, [this queen Yasodharā] together with me gave great feasts to fifty million plus ninety million Buddhas who are greater than the gods.]

"Great King Suddhōdana, this Queen Yasodharā together with me in *saṃsāra* fulfilled the requirements needed for Enlightenment, and over a long period of time practiced the Ten Perfections such as Generosity and Moral practices. Hear it then from me," he said.

adhikāraṃ mahā mayhaṃ mahā rājā sunohi me
**sasthī kōti satāni Buddhā sattha kōti satā nica*
ētesaṃ deva devānaṃ mahādānaṃ pavatthayiṃ[36]

*[gave gifts to one hundred and thirty *kōti* times a hundred, plus a hundred *kōti* Buddhas][37]

"Great King Suddhōdana, This queen Yasodharā together with me in *saṃsāra* fulfilled the requirements for Enlightenment, and over a long period of time practiced the Ten Perfections such as Generosity and Moral Practices. Hear it then from me," he said. "This Queen Yasodharā gave great offerings of alms to one hundred and thirty thousand million *kela*[38] times a hundred Buddhas, Enlightened Ones, preeminent among gods.

adhikāraṃ mahā mayhaṃ mahā rājā sunohi me
**asiti kōti satāni Buddhā nauti kōti sathā nica.*
ētesaṃ deva devānaṃ mahā dānaṃ pavattyiṃ

---

35. Stanzas 72–80 of the PA are given in successive verses. A paraphrase, not a translation, of each verse follows. The verses are repetitive and only the numbers increase to give a sense of the enormity of her generosity. I have only attempted to translate the numbers stated in each verse.

36. Since the verse is the same and only the numbers change, I give only the numbers.

37. Again the verse is repeated, but in the explanation the term *kela* is used to translate *kōti*; the terms are thus interchangeable.

38. *kela* is considered equal to 10,000,000 but is also used as a general term for an infinite number. It is used interchangeably with the word *kōti*, which has a similar meaning both of a specific number and an infinite amount.

*[gave gifts to one hundred and eighty *kōti* times a hundred and another hundred *kōti* Buddhas]

"Great King Suddhōdana, born of the Sun clan, hear from me now how this Queen Yasodharā when she was with me in *saṃsāra*, fulfilled the requirements for Enlightenment," he said. "In the world age known as the *sāramaddha* era this queen Yasodharā herself gave great feasts of alms to fourteen hundred *kela* of Supreme Buddhas, Enlightened Ones, preeminent among gods [who lived in that era.]

adhikāraṃ mahā mayhaṃ mahārājā suṇohi me
**ekā sataṃ kōti satānica*
ētesaṃ deva devānaṃ mahā dānaṃ pavattayiṃ[39]

*[gave to one hundred *kōti* times a hundred Buddhas]

"Great King Suddhōdana who comes down from the clan of the Mahāsammata, this blessed woman Yasodharā accompanied me though *saṃsāra*, fulfilling the requirements needed for Enlightenment, and over a long period fulfilled the Ten Perfections such as Generosity and Moral practices. Hear this from me" he said.

"In the world age known as the *sāramaddha* era this chief Queen Yasodharā herself gave great offerings of alms to ninety *kela* of Supreme Buddhas, preeminent among gods.

"This Queen Yasodharā gave great feasts of alms to one hundred and seventy *kela* times a hundred Enlightened Ones, Lord Protectors, preeminent among gods.

adhikāraṃ mahā mayhaṃ mahā rājā sunohi me
**kōti sata sahassāni honti lokassagga nāyakā*
ētesaṃ deva devānaṃ mahā dānaṃ pavattayiṃ

*[gave to one hundred thousand *koti* Buddhas]

"Great King Suddhōdana, this chief Queen Yasodharā accompanied me through the *saṃsaric* cycles fulfilling the requirements for Enlightenment and over a long

39. This stanza is not in the PA and is not paraphrased or explained in the text.

period of time practiced the Ten Perfections such as Generosity and Moral Practices.[40] Hear this from me" he said.

"This Queen Yasodharā gave great feasts of alms to one hundred thousand *kela* of Enlightened Ones, preeminent among gods.

adhikāraṃ mahā mayhaṃ mahā rājā suṇnohi me
**nava kōti sahassāni aparelokagga nāyako*
ētesaṃ deva devānaṃ mahā dānaṃ pavattayiṃ

*[gave to nine *kōti* times a thousand Buddhas]

"Great King Suddhōdana who ruled according to the ten principles of kingship, this mother of Rāhula together with me fulfilled the requirements for Enlightenment and over a long period of time practiced the Ten Perfections such as Generosity and Moral Practices. Hear this from me. This Great Queen Yasodharā herself gave great feasts of alms to nine *kela* times a thousand Buddhas who had escaped from *saṃsāra.*

adhikāraṃ mahā mayhaṃ mahārājā sunohi me
**kōti satasahassāni pañcā sīti mahesinaṃ*
pañcāsīti kōti satā sattavīsati kōtiyo
ētesaṃ deva devānaṃ mahā dānaṃ pavattāyiṃ

*[gave to one hundred thousand times five thousand *kōti,* plus one *koti* two thousand five hundred Buddhas]

"Great King Suddhōdana, banner of the Sākya clan, this Queen Yasodharā together with me fulfilled the requirements for Enlightenment and over a long period of time fulfilled the Perfections such as Generosity. Hear this from me," he said.

"This Queen Yasodharā, gave great feasts of alms to one *lakh* five thousand *kōti* and for ten million two thousand five hundred Buddhas, Enlightened Ones, preeminent among gods, preeminent among Brahmas. Great King Suddhōdana, lord, chief of a good lineage, this mother of Rāhula, together with me fulfilled

---

40. Verses tend to be repetitive with very slight variations. The effect is perhaps intended to be cumulative.

the requirements needed for Enlightenment over a long period of time in *saṃsāra*. Hear this from me," he said.

"This mother of Rāhula herself, gave great feasts of alms to about sixteen *kela* of *paccēka*[41] Buddhas, Noble Ones, lords of all two-footed beings.

Adhikāra sahāmāyāhaṃ mahārāja sunohi
**asītikōti satāni Buddhā nautikōti satānica*
ētesaṃ deva devānaṃ mahā dānaṃ pavattayi[42]

*[gave to eighty *kōti* and one hundred plus ninety *kōti* times one hundred Buddhas]

"Great King Suddhōdana, this Queen Yasodharā together with me in *saṃsāra* fulfilled the requirements for Enlightenment over a long period of time, and engaged in the Ten Meritorious Actions such as Generosity and Moral Practices. Hear it from me. This Queen Yasodharā gave great feasts of alms to those Buddhas and to their *arahat* disciples, beings rid of all desires" he said.

The Lord Buddha, proclaimed thus to his father, King Suddhōdana, of the firm resolve and past commitment of Queen Yasodharā, in fulfilling the meritorious acts of Generosity and Moral Practices. [He made this declaration] as if revealing a treasure hidden in his father Suddhōdana's own royal grounds, or as if because of the meritorious powers of a world conquering king, the sea parted revealing seven precious gems, or as if a door opened to a room decorated with [beautiful] paintings.

Thus did the Buddha, Lord of the World, give an account of her past acts to his father the king, and to the doubting gods and men. Queen Yasodharā then stated her earlier resolution before the Buddha in a lion's roar and the crowds of gods and Brahmas gathered instantly, raised their hands in worship and again and again acclaimed "*sādhu*" (well done.)

Putting aside doubts, all the gods and humans, men and women who witnessed her miracles, with happy minds instantly made a fervent wish[43] to obtain

---

41. *Paccēka* Buddhas are those enlightened ones who do not preach the dhamma to others.

42. In the text I have, this is not set in stanza form but as a continuing paragraph of prose. There are also variations in the text that suggest further errors. However, as it is clearly a Pali stanza, I have put it in italics.

43. I translate the Buddhist concept of *prartanā* as Fervent Wish.

the blessings of virtue, the blessings of respect, the blessings of good consequences, the blessings of wisdom, the blessings of meritorious deeds and the blessings of the nectar of *nirvāṇa.* In this manner, when the *Thēri* Yasodharā worshipped the Buddha, obtained forgiveness, and requested permission [to leave], the Buddha, aware that now the residents of all Three Worlds knew of the power of the *Thēri* Yasodharā's great Acts of Merit and her enormous miraculous powers, thought it was time to give her leave to go.

"Great Senior Nun Yasodharā, most worthy and most blessed, there is no need to forgive one like you who has obtained the nectar of *nirvāṇa.* However, as it is the tradition in the world I grant forgiveness to you Yasodharā" he said.

"Besides *Thēri* Yasodharā, the setting of the Buddha's own sun, namely achieving *nirvāṇa* will occur in twenty-four months," he declared.

Then, as if a large branch from the wish fulfilling tree [*kalpa vrukśha*] that was the Buddha had now died, he said, "Proceed to *nirvāṇa.*"

She worshipped the Buddha, bade farewell, circumambulated him three times, stepped back, and raising both hands in worship said, "Lord, just as the water that reaches the sea does not flow back into the river and as the water that goes into the mouth of Makara [sea monster] does not return to the sea, so I who never left you over an infinite period of time, will now go away and not be seen again." So saying, as if a universal monarch's jewel was [suddenly] hidden or as if the sun had set, she left for the nunnery.

When she had left, on the Buddha's advice the monks and laity gathered there followed her. She went to the nunnery and that night attained *nirvāṇa* they said.

Later the Buddha with a host of gods, Brahmas and a huge crowd [of people] gathered and performed the funeral rites. Thereafter the Buddha took the relics and had a *stūpa*[44] constructed, offered flowers and lights, and instructed the residents of Dambadiva to make daily offerings in order to acquire the blessings of heaven and *nirvāṇa.* Thus, because of that great *stūpa* all men could perform Acts of Merit and arrive at the city of heaven and the city of *nirvāṇa* and escape the sufferings of *saṃsāra.*

Devoted men and women should therefore listen to this *Yasodharāpadānaya*, keep it in mind, perform Acts of Merit according to their means, acquire the blessings of this world, the world of the gods and Brahmas, the blessings of

44. A *stūpa* is a bubble-shaped structure constructed to house the relics of the Buddha, Buddhist monks, and nuns.

wealth and goods and finally strive to see the Maitreya Buddha[45] and attain the blessings of the nectar of *nirvāṇa.*

Here ends the *Yasodharāpadānaya.*

Mangalonāma nāmena upasanthehi bhikhunā
Mettheyya sabba dassāmi
Pottakam likitam idam Siddhi rastu

[I, a fully ordained monk named Mangala
have written this book
and transfer Merit to all creatures.]

45. Maitreya is the name of the next Buddha, the one who will follow the Buddha Gautama.

APPENDIX

A Review of the Palm Leaf Manuscripts of the *Yasodharāvata* in the National Museum Library, Colombo, and the British Museum Library, London

I have located eight palm leaf manuscripts entitled *Yasodharāvata* (The Story of Yasodharā). Five are in verse and three in prose. Of the five manuscripts in verse, four are different from the poem *Yasodharāvata* (A) translated by me. They deal with different events in Yasodharā's life, with different emphases. So do the prose versions. Though titled *Yasodharāvata*, the prose manuscripts seem to be versions of the *Yasodarāpadānaya* text.

Yasodharāvata kavi (PL 1)
BR 66 04
BO N 269
29 leaves, 196 verses
British Museum Library

Of the palm leaf manuscripts of poems entitled *Yasodharāvata,* the earliest is possibly this text from the Hugh Neville Collection in the British Museum Library. It is called the *Yasodharāvata kavi* (The Story of Yasodharā in Verse) and consists of 196 verses on twenty-nine palm leaves. Verse 182 states, however, that it was composed in 210 verses. Since there are four verses transcribed on one side and three on the other of each palm leaf, we can assume that the two last leaves (a total of fourteen verses) are missing. I shall call it PL (1).

As mentioned earlier, in verses 183 and 184 the identity of the author is given as the eldest daughter of a king named Bopiti of Udapalagama. It gives a date of composition as the Buddha era 1895. K. D. Somadasa interprets the verse to mean "that it was composed in 1895 of the Buddhist era which would place it as 1352 CE in the reign of King Buveneka Bahu IV of Gangasiripura."[1] The present manuscript seems to have been transcribed at a much later date and by a very unskilled scribe, judging from the badly formed letters. Since the Neville collection was made about eighty-five years ago, the manuscript itself may be between 100 and 150 years old.

This poem is quite different from the popular folk version *Yasodharāvata* (A). It gives an extended biography of Yasodharā as linked to the Buddha narrative. An early verse describes her as the young woman who makes a Fervent Wish to the Buddha Dīpankara that when the hermit Sumeda is to become a Buddha (many eons hence) she should be born as his wife (verse 10). That is an incident that is not referred to in *Yasodharavata* (A).

Verses 11–13 tell of her birth as the wife of the Bōdhisattva Vessantara, living in the forest with him where he gives away their children. There is no account of the mother's lament that many Vessantara folk texts have, only a reference to the main known story.

Verses 13–17 refer to their subsequent life in the Tusita heaven and the Bōdhisattva's decision to be born on earth in Queen Māyā's womb.

Verses 18–22 are part of the known Buddha narrative of the Bōdhisattva's birth and childhood—not different from that described in *Yasodharāvata* (A).

Verses 23–36 tell of Yasodharā's selection to be the bride of Prince Sidhartha, and give an extended description of her beauty and their happy life until his twenty-ninth year.

Verses 37–46 take up the narrative of the Bōdhisattva's decision to leave his wife and home, followed by the period spent in his quest for enlightenment. There is no emotional farewell on the part of the Bōdhisattva as in *Yasodharāvata* (A). Two verses briefly relate his visit to see his wife and newborn son. Nor is there a lament by Yasodharā on his departure as in the *Yasodharāvata* (A) text.

The next event describes the Buddha's return to Kapilavastu and the sermons to his kinfolk. No reference is made to Yasodharā's refusal to go hear him preach.

Twenty verses (50–70) deal with Yasodharā sending her son to meet his father and the child Rāhula's meeting with the Buddha.

---

1. K. D. Somadasa, *Catalogue of the Hugh Neville Collection of Sinhalese Manuscripts in the British Library*, vol. 3, London: Pali Text Society, 1990.

Verses 71 and 72 tell of Rāhula's ordination, and Yasodharā's great grief at the loss of her son.

Verse 74 deals with her determination to become a nun and obtain the gift of ordination that all her kinsmen and her son have now received.

Verses 75–85 describe her walk to the city of Kōsala and Visāla to be ordained.

Verses 86–89 show her following the rules of discipline and finally becoming an *arahat.* Then because of her great charisma resulting from her past Acts of Merit she is surrounded by laity who bring her offerings. She decides to leave the nunnery and go elsewhere (perhaps seeking more privacy).

Verses 90–172 describe the last day of her life and her visit to the Buddha. The events recorded are from the *Yasodharāpadānaya* rendered now in verse.

Verses 173–181 describe Yasodharā's funeral and the building of a *stūpa* over her ashes. The Buddha is described as present at that event. They seem to indicate the end of her story.

Verse 182 refers to the number of verses in the poem.

Verses 183–184 give the identity of the author and the date of composition.

The subsequent verses are a kind of traditional closure with praises to the Buddha, transference of Merit to the gods, and a request to be forgiven for any shortcomings in the poem.

PL 1 (B)
Fol: 55
SK v
A M 7
Talipot fol. 13½" × 1½"
National Museum Library, Colombo

This manuscript in the National Museum Library in Colombo is almost identical with PL 1 in the British Museum Library so I shall call it PL 1 (B).

PL 1 (B) ends at verse 182 in the PL 1 text. While the PL 1 text says it was composed in 210 verses, PL 1(B) says it was composed in 207 verses. Neither manuscript has the full complement of the verses stated in the texts, so palm leaves are missing from both. PL 1(B) starts from verse 22 of the PL 1 text. It is clear that the text of PL 1(B) is intended to end at verse 182 as it is followed by the prose statement, "By the merit I have acquired by writing down this Yasodharā Jātaka may I be reborn in the time of the Buddha Maitreya."

The text of PL 1, by contrast, goes on in the next two verses 183 and 184 to give a specific identity to the author as the daughter of the King Bopiti and a date of its composition. It is possible that the last few verses of PL 1 (which give the author's identity) were (perhaps intentionally) omitted by the transcriber of PL 1(B). Of the two versions, it is likely that manuscript PL 1 was the earlier manuscript as the claim made in PL1B is that of being the transcriber and not of being author.

PL 1 claims authorship and a much earlier date, so it is probably the earlier text.

Two other palm leaf manuscript poems are also titled *Yasodharāvata* (Story of Yasodharā), but they too are different poems, not versions of the popular *Yasodharāvata* (A). They seem to be fragments of the same manuscript, so I shall call them PL 2 and PL 2 (B).

PL 2
85.0.19
W.A.D.S./317
Talipot fol. 7" × 1½"
National Museum Library, Colombo

There are thirty one verses of four lines on a page; each line is six inches long.

The poem begins with the Enlightenment of the Buddha and the defeat of Māra.

Verses 1–3 relate the defeat of Māra.

Verses 4–16 describe Māra's daughters and their efforts to seduce the Buddha. They even take on the guise of Yasodharā suckling her child Rāhula. I shall give translations of a few lines to convey a sense of the content of the poem.

Verse 11
You have had a son born to you
He is named Rāhula
King Suddhōdana thinks you are dead
Come with us, King Suddhōdhana commands you.

Is it not a sin for you to abandon your son?

Verse 15
Gold earrings in the ears
A pearl chain at the waist
If only you will look at us
You will fall in love with us.
Thus they danced around the lord.

Verse 16
There are many other husbands in this world
They too love their women
My beauty lights up the world
Still he does not look or speak to us.

Verse 17
A hundred rooms have been built for you
Your queen awaits you
Suddhōdana your father waits for you

Verse 20
Having become a Buddha why do you sit there
Having become a Buddha should you not enjoy pleasure
All alone here we weep
Does your heart not melt for our many sorrows?

Verses 21–24 all refer to the Buddha's firm resolution and victory over Māra.

Verse 31
The three (daughters of Māra) descended from *sakvala*
They went away defeated
Dear brother don't be sad for us
We battled hard but you did not look at us.

This poem is really about the attempts by Māra's daughters to seduce the Bōdhisattva. Perhaps because at one time they take on the appearance of Yasodharā and her son Rāhula this work has been wrongfully titled *Yasodharāvata* by some later scribe. There is very little about Yasodharā in this poem, though it is catalogued and titled as *Yasodharāvata* among the palm leaf manuscripts of the National Museum Library in Sri Lanka.

PL 2 (B) begins with what is the last verse of PL 2. It ends with what is verse 2 in PL 2. The two manuscripts are clearly the same poem, but again PL 2 (B) has been collated wrongly or the same poem has been transcribed by different people at different times and recorded as two texts.

PL 3
85 R 28
W.A.D.S/648
Talipot fol. 6

11 Talipot leaves 9" × 1½"
4 lines, 8" long on a side
21 verses
National Museum Library Colombo

This was the only palm leaf manuscript I found where some of the verses were identical with those in the *Yasodharāvata* (A). The manuscript as it now stands begins at verse 105 (of the *Yasodharāvata* (A) text) and ends at verse 117. The leaves seem jumbled.

The present order in the manuscript as compared with *Yasodharāvata* (A) is as follows.

v.105–108 (two leaves)
v.113–116 (two leaves)
v.109–112 (two leaves)
v.93–100 (four leaves)
v.101–104 (two leaves—missing)
v.105–108 (two leaves)
v.109–112 (two leaves)
v.113–116 (two leaves)
v. 117 (single leaf)

When rearranged, the manuscript does have twenty-one consecutive verses from 93 to 117 with just two leaves missing. We can regard this manuscript as either an excerpted version of the longer poem the *Yasodharāvata* (A) or the popular folk poem as being an expanded version of this earlier text. Since two leaves are already missing from this manuscript, it is possible that the first part of the text was also lost. It is also possible that the poem consisted of just ten verses of Yasodharā's lament, followed by the verses on the Bōdhisattva's life after leaving the palace and Yasodharā's final death. While many of the verses of lament could have been accumulations or additions over time, it seems very unlikely that the first part of the Buddha narrative, which gives a context to Yasodharā's lament, would not have been part of the original poem. I prefer therefore to hypothesize that this is a manuscript fragment. Verse 117 describing the *stūpa* built as a commemorative monument to Yasodharā is on a single leaf and therefore is clearly the final verse. The mixup in the order of the verses could have resulted from the careless tying up of the leaves—something that easily happens since the manuscripts are not bound and pages are not numbered. The palm leaves are strung together on a cord and are meant to be read in their sequence, but when the cords disintegrate, the leaves fall apart and are often carelessly retied.

It is significant that verse 117 of *Yasodharāvata* (A) that seemed even on a casual reading to be the logical end of the Yasodharā poem does in fact form a break. If the palm leaf version is a fairly early text, then it is likely that verses 118–124 of the *Yasodharāvata* (A) were a later stratum or layer. They have a very different metrical structure and deal with Yasodharā's miraculous powers after she becomes an *arahat*. (In the Yasodharā story this occurs before she dies—not after, as the addition to the poem implies.)

There are three other palm leaf manuscripts also called *Yasodharāvata* in the National Museum library in Colombo, but they are in prose.

PL 6
Fol. 17 (ka–kaa)
6 F 3
Talipot leaves 19¼" × 3½"
7 lines 17" long on a leaf
National Museum Library, Colombo

The letters here are well formed since the manuscript was very likely transcribed by a monk.

The content of the manuscript is close to the *Yasodharāpadānaya* text. It is in Sinhala prose with Pali verses intermixed. There is a long account of Yasodharā Thēri's earlier lives—as told by her to the Buddha, on the day before she dies. The text mentions three kinds of wives that are bad:

Vadaka bhāriyāva (troublesome wife)
Cōra bhāriyāva (stealthy or secretive wife)
Swāmi bhāriyāva (masterful wife)

And four kinds of wives that are good:

Māthru bhāriyāva (motherly wife)
Bhagini bhāriyava (meritorious or blessed wife)
Sriyā bhāriyāva (pleasing and lovely wife)
Dāsi bhāriyāva (wife who serves)

Yasodharā claims that in their past lives together she has been all the latter four types of wives to the Buddha. [These categories do not appear in the Yasodharāpadāna text either in the Pali or the Sinhala version I translate.]

She goes on to claim (as in the *apadāna* text) that in various past births he has given her away as *dāna* (generous gift) to other people, pawned her (*ukas keruva*), endowed her to others (*pāvādunna*), and gifted her to others (*dan dunna*), but she never blamed him for it. She also sacrificed her life for him.

The text ends with an account of her funeral attended by gods and men and by the Buddha, and the building of an enormous *stūpa* for her relics. It is significant that verse 117 in the *Yasodharāvata* (A) also ends at that point.

PL 7
6 F 3
Microfilm: Reel No. 57
(From the library of the Potgul Vihara, Hanguranketa)
National Museum Library, Colombo

The text states that this is the account of Yasodharā Thēri and the miracles she performed as stated in chapter 31 of the *Pūjāvaliya,* a thirteenth century text by the monk Mayurāpada.

PL 8
Microfilm made on 1986/03/08
Reel No. 118
36 leaves
(From the Yāpahūwa Raja Mahā Vihāra library)
National Museum Library, Colombo

The text states that it was written partly in 1743 and completed in 1744 by Āgalle Vidāne. The author's name indicates that the writer was not a monk but a lay member of the local intelligentsia. It also seems to borrow from the Sinhala work, the *Jinālankāra.*

The text begins with a long account by the monk Ānanda at the *Sangāyana* (First Council) and his account of the life of the Buddha. There is a short last section on Yasodharā that seems to be from the *Yasodharāpadāna*. Ir covers much of the same materal and recounts all that she did for the Buddha because of her love for him. Pali verses are intermixed in the text.

Glossary

Amaravati

She was the wise wife of the famous scholar Mahausada in one of the birth stories (jātaka) of the Bōdhisattva. Literally means "the undying one."

Anāgāmin

It is the third stage in the four stages of the Path to *nirvāṇa*. The term is also translated as a "nonreturner"; one who will not be reborn again in *saṃsāra*.

Anēpiḍu (p. Anātapinḍika)

It is the Sinhala name for the nobleman Anātapinḍika who was a lay disciple and patron of the Buddha and built the Jētavana monastery.

Anotatta

In Hindu Buddhist cosmology, this is a mythical lake at the foot of the mountain called Mēru at the center of the universe.

Arahat

Is a "noble one" or "Enlightened One" who has reached the last of the four stages of the Path to *nirvāṇa.*

Bhāvanā (meditation)

One of the three aspects of Buddhist practice and essential if one is to reach *nirvāṇa.*

Bimbā

Another name for Yasodharā. Bimbā is the older usage.

Bōdhi tree

It is the tree under which the Buddha attained Enlightenment and so is revered by Buddhists. It is a species of ficus (*ficus religiosa*) called *Bō* in Sinhala.

Bōdhisattva

Is an aspirant to becoming a Buddha. One who cultivates Virtues or Perfections (*pāramitā*) during innumerable existences in *saṃsāra* and finally attains Enlightenment as a Buddha.

Bōsat

This is another term for the Bōdhisattva common in Sinhala literature.

Brahma heavens

This is the heaven where the radiant brahmas as they are called, dwell. There are two categories: the corporeal brahmas and the formless brahmas. They are heavenly beings and of a higher order of gods than *dēvas* as they are free from sensual passions. According to the Buddha, even Brahma heavens, like all other heavens, are not eternal. They, like the human world, are subject to final destruction.

Buddha

An Enlightened One who by his own wisdom and insight has realized the state of *nirvāṇa*. See also Three forms of Enlightenment.

Buddha rays (s. *budu räs*)

The rays believed to emanate from a Buddha's person.

Chain of Causation (p. *paticca samuppāda*)

The term given to a well-known Buddhist doctrine translated as "Dependent Origination." It sums up the principal causes of existence in their order of succession. It also embodies the Buddhist statement of a solution to the problem of suffering and so is a fundamental part of the teachings.

Consciousness (p. *viňňāna*)

As a metaphysical concept in the Buddhist teachings it has eighty-nine subdivisions under three broad categories: Meritorious thoughts (*kusala viňňāna*); Demeritorious thoughts (*akusala viňňāna*); and Indifferent thoughts (*avyākata viňňāna*).

Canna

He was the minister and friend of the Bōdhisattva throughout *saṃsāra,* and accompanied him when he left the palace in search of Enlightenment.

Crore

Is equivalent to ten million or one hundred *lakhs.*

Dambadiva

It is the Sinhala name for India; a variation of Jambudipa, which is the more formal usage.

Damsak Pävatum Sutta (p. *Dhammacakkappavattana Sūtta*)

It means literally the stanzas to set in motion the wheel of the doctrine or the sermon on the "Establishment of the Doctrine." It was the first sermon the Buddha preached after attaining Enlightenment and it contains the fundamentals of the Doctrine such as the Four Noble Truths.

Dāna

Generosity or the "Act of Giving." It is one of the three ethical principles fundamental to Buddhism. The other two are *sīla* (moral conduct) and *bhāvana* (meditation).

Defilements (s. & sk. *Kleśa*)

It is also translated as Impurities. There are ten Impurities or Defilements: craving, hate, ignorance, vanity, erroneous beliefs, doubt, sloth, arrogance, lack of shame to sin, and lack of fear to sin.

Demerit (s. *akusal*)

Bad or wrong acts that have negative karmic consequences.

Deveramvehera

It is the Sinhala term for the Jetavana, the monastery built by the nobleman Anātapinḍika. It was located near the city of Sāvatti (s. *Sävät*) and was one of the major monasteries where the Buddha spent the longest time during the years of his teaching.

Dhamma (s.& sk. *dharma*)

It is the term used to describe the fundamental law or Doctrine of existence and salvation as expounded by a Buddha. It is also commonly used for Buddhist discourses, conversations, or teachings of the Buddha Gautama.

Divine Eye (s. *diväsa*)

Enlightened Ones or *arahats* have the power of clairvoyance, thought reading, and the recollection of their own and other's past lives in earlier births. Acquiring the Divine Eye is one of the supernormal powers obtained by *arahats* by intense meditation and the attaining of Trance States. I translate it also as All-seeing Eye.

Divine Ear (s. *diva kan*)

Clairaudience, another of the supernormal powers obtained by attaining Trance States.

Dīpankara

It is the name for one of the former Buddhas. Buddhists believe that there were many Buddhas who lived and preached the Doctrine in different eons across *saṃsāric* time. Buddha Dīpankara preceded the present Buddha Gautama. He was one of a long line of Buddhas.

Dipavaṃsa

A fourth century CE chronicle in Pali, but believed to be from earlier Sinhala sources. It records a history of the kings of the island and the establishment of Buddhism.

Eight Meditative Attainments (p. *aṭṭha samāpatti*)

A Buddhist philosophical concept that refers to Eight Attainments or endowments or modes of abstraction induced by ecstatic meditation.

Elu

Is the name for an early form of the Sinhala language.

Enlightenment

Is the Buddhist term for supreme knowledge or understanding. It is the bliss that arises from extinguishing the fires of lust, ill will, and delusion. It is the ultimate goal for all Buddhists. See also *Nirvāṇa*.

Fervent Rebirth Wish (s. *prārtanā* or *pätuma*)

Buddhism has no provision for prayer as the Buddha does not claim to be a deity. Therefore, a *prārtanā* or wish for something in the next life is the nearest equivalent. It is, however, often more than a wish or a prayer. It is a moral resolve to achieve a specific goal in the next life such as a Bōdhisattva's *prārtanā* to become a Buddha, made over a succession of rebirths. The wish is often made after the performance of a pious act. As it is most often related to the next or future lives I have translated it as Fervent Rebirth Wish.

Four Guardian Gods

For Sri Lanka they are the gods Vishnu, Kataragama (also known as Skanda), Saman, and Nāta and they are believed to be protectors of the country and the Buddhist religion.

Gajaman Nōna

Is a woman poet who lived and wrote in the nineteenth century.

Garuda

Is an enormous mythical bird that feeds on snakes.

Gautama

Is the name given to the Buddha whose dispensation is the present, therefore he is also referred to as "our Buddha." He is but one of a long line of Buddhas and will be followed by the Buddha Maitreyya.

Gav

Is a specific measure of distance equivalent to four miles. I decided to translate it by the more general term "league."

Gōtami

Prajāpati Gōtami was the foster mother of the Bōdhisattva. According to the Buddha narrative in the Theravada tradition, Siddharta's mother, Queen Māyā, died after childbirth. Prajāpati Gōtami was her sister who then became the Buddha's surrogate mother and the second wife of Suddhōdana. She was also the one who finally persuaded the Buddha to establish an order of Buddhist nuns of which she became the head.

Jātaka stories

These are stories of the past lives of the Bōdhisattva during the years he spent in *saṃsāra*. They are a compendium of 550 birth stories (the exact number of extant stories is a little less) that have come down through the centuries and illustrate important aspects of Buddhist doctrine.

Kalpa

The term is used to suggest vast periods of time but of lesser duration than an *asankya*. All universes are subjected to a process of destruction and renovation. A *mahākalpa* is the period that elapses from the commencement or restoration of a universe to its complete destruction. I have translated it as eon for lack of a better term. (See also Uncountables).

Karma

Literally means action or deed. Thus, good and bad *karma* refers to Acts of Merit or Demerit and their consequences. There are two broad categories of *karma: patisandi karma* are actions that give rise to only one result and nothing thereafter; *pavatti karma* are actions whose multiple consequences occur in a succession of future rebirths..

Kantaka

Is the horse that the Bōdhisattva rode when he left his palace to take up the life of an ascetic.

Kavi kola

This was the term used for printed pamphlets of poems that were sold cheaply at market fairs and were mainly sung

Kusa

The Bōdhisattva was born as a king but was extremely ugly because of a negative action in a past birth. He fell in love with the beautiful princess Pabāvati who was horrified at his ugliness and rejected him. He had to resort to all kinds of stratagems to win her.

Kuvēni

In the origin myth of the island, Kuvēni was the queen of Lanka at the time when Prince Vijaya (the mythical ancestor of the Sinhala people) came to the island. She falls in love with him and marries him and gives him the kingdom. He later sends her into exile in order to marry queens from Indian royal families.

Lakh

It is the term for one hundred thousand (100,000).

"Lion roar"

The baby Bōdhisattva is supposed to have given such a roar at birth to indicate that he was to become a Supreme Buddha.

Madri devi

She was the wife of the Bōdhisattva when he was born as King Vessantara. She followed him to the forest when he left his kingdom for a life of asceticism. However, when she finds he has given away her two children to a mendicant, she is devastated with grief and combs the forest weeping and looking for them.

Mahavaṃsa

This was a sixth century CE chronicle that gives the history of the establishment of Buddhism in the island and an account of the kings who supported Buddhism.

Maitreyya

Is the name of the Bōdhisattva presently in the Tusita heaven who will be the next Buddha.

Māra

Māra was the king/god of the demons who tried his best to distract and prevent the Buddha from attaining Enlightenment under the *Bō* tree. The term has come to be synonymous with death and destruction.

Māyā

Māyā is the name of the chief queen of Suddhōdana and mother of the Bōdhisattva Siddharta. The word means illusion in Pali.

Merit

It is a term used for the Buddhist concept of "good" that is defined in terms of actions. Thus, good acts are Acts of Merit (s. *pin*). Evil is defined in terms of wrong acts or Acts of Demerit (s. *pau*).

Muni

Another term used for the Buddha.

Nāga

Is the Sinhala word for a hooded snake. In the Buddhist story, they have a special place as creatures that helped, supported, and sustained the Buddha's Doctrine. One of them, a cobra, sheltered the Buddha when he was seated in meditation under the *Bōdhi* tree. The world of the *nāgas* in Buddhist mythology is located in the nether regions below the rock that supports Mount Meru, below the earth but above the underworld or hell. The Buddha preached to them and many were converted to the Path.

Nirvāṇa

Is the term for Supreme Enlightenment, the cessation of all desire, ill will, and delusion and the end to the continuous process of Rebirth. It is the ultimate goal for a Buddhist.

Pabāvati

She was an extraordinarily beautiful woman who was tricked into marrying the ugly King Kusa. When she discovers what has happened, she leaves her husband and returns to her natal home. Kusa follows her there, disguised as a menial servant, and finally wooes and wins her.

Paccēka Buddha (s. *pase Budu*)

Sometimes also called the silent Buddhas because, though they have attained Enlightenment, they do not preach or teach the Doctrine to others.

Path and Fruits (s. & sk. *Mārga-phala*)

The stages that lead to Enlightenment in Buddhism are termed *marga* (path) and *phala* (fruits). These are the four stages of the path and their specific forms of realization or fruits. The first stage is that of the *sotāpanna* (s. *sōvān*) Stream-Enterer, one who has entered the stream of salvation; the second is *sakadāgāmi* (the Once Returner) who can be born once more in the human world before attaining *nirvāṇa*; the third is *anāgāmi* (the nonreturner) who will not be born again as a human before he attains *nirvāṇa*; and the fourth is *arahat*, one who has attained Enlightenment. With each stage comes also an accompanying realization or fruits of that stage.

Perfections

There are ten virtues or Perfections (*pāramita*) that one must tirelessly cultivate throughout one's *saṃsāric* existences to become a Buddha. They are Generosity, Morality, Renunciation, Wisdom, Effort, Patience, Truthfulness, Resolution, Kindness, and Equanimity. Each can be further subdivided into the ordinary, the inferior, and the unlimited form—hence the reference sometimes to the Thirty Perfections.

Rāhula

He is the only son of Siddharta and Yasodharā. It was predicted that on the day he was born his father would leave on his quest for Enlightenment. Later Rāhula too becomes a monk in the Buddha's order. The word means "bond" or "fetter"

Sahampati

Is the name for the Lord of the Brahma heavens. It was he who made the first offering to the Bōdhisattva of the eight requisites necessary for a monk when he is about to set out on his quest for Enlightenment.

Sala (s. *sal*)

It is a flowering tree found in North India. The Buddha was born in a *sāla* grove, according to the Buddha story.

Sakra

Sakra is the king of the gods (*devas*) and a supporter of the Buddha's Doctrine.

Sākya

Is the name of the clan to which Siddharta belonged. It was a *ksatriya* (princely) not a b*rahmin* (priestly) caste.

Saṃsāra

The continuous cycle of birth, decay, and death that Buddhists consider characterizes the human condition and is the cause of suffering. Enlightenment provides release from the *saṃsāric* cycle.

Sävät

Is the Sinhala term for the city of Sāvatti where the Buddha spent time teaching his Doctrine.

Säriyut

Is the Sinhala form of the name Sāriputta who was one of the Buddha's chief disciples.

Sāsana

Is an inclusive term for the Buddha's teachings, the order of the monks and the lay devotees. The nearest equivalent in English would be the concept of the church as in the "church of Christ." However, the connotations of the term church are so Christian that I have refrained from using it.

Siddharta

The name of the Bōdhisattva who was born a prince of the Sākya clan in his last birth prior to his becoming a Buddha.

Sothiya

Is the name of a Brahmin who, according to the Buddha story, made an offering of *kusa* grass to the Buddha as he was about to take his seat under the *Bōdhi* tree. The *Bōdhisattva* used the grass as a cushion for his seat under the *Bō* tree where he remained until he attained Enlightenment.

Spiritual Attainments (s. *nava lovutura daham*)

It is also translated as the Nine Transcendental or Supramundane States. They consist of the attainments of the four stages of the path, the four fruits of the path and *nirvāṇa.*

Stūpa

A bubble-shaped structure in which the ashes or other relics of the Buddha or *arahats* are enshrined and buried.

Sudhōvan

This is the Sinhala form of the name Sudhōdana, the father of the Bōdhisattva.

Sumedha

He was the hermit who lay across a marshy rivulet so that the Buddha Dīpankara could walk on him and not muddy his feet. He then made a Fervent Wish (*prārtanā*) to become a Buddha himself. Many eons later, he became the Buddha Gautama.

Three worlds

In Buddhist cosmology they refer to heaven, or the home of the gods (*deva*); the human world; and the spirit world, hell or the world of lust (*kāma*).

Trance states (s. *dhyana*)

States achieved through the attainment of full concentration and deep meditation during which there is the complete, though temporary, suspension of the five-fold sense activities. However, this state of consciousness is also a state of full alertness and lucidity.

Trance state of Cessation (p. *nirōdhasamāpatti*)

One of the many categories of Trance States that can be achieved by concentrated contemplation.

Uncountables (s. *asankeyya;* p. *asankya*)

It literally means unnumbered or uncountable. To indicate vast periods of *saṃsāric* time Buddhist cosmology deals in *asankya* (uncountables or immeasurables) and in *kalpa (*loosely translated as eons), all of which are ironically counted, thereby both extending the concept of infinity and making it in a strange way quantifiable and comprehensible.

Vaṃsakatā

They are stories or histories of lineages. Also used as a general term for histories.

Vädda

A term used to describe hunters who lived in the forests.

Vessantara

He was the Bōdhisattva in his birth as a king known for his boundless generosity. He refused no request. He gave away his kingdom, wealth, and even his wife and two children.

Vidurāsana (p. *Vajrāsana*)

Is the name for the immovable seat of the god Sakra. When the Bōdhisattva sits under the *Bōdhi* tree determined not to move until he has achieved full Enlightenment, the seat is therefore termed a *vajrāsana* like Sakra's immovable seat.

Vilāpa

Chants or laments that relate an account of loss or an expression of deep grief.

Vitti kavi

They are poems that narrate events or incidents of significance.

Vivaraṇa

Literally means a declaration, but in the Buddhist literature it has come to mean an assurance that a specific event will come to pass in a future life. I translate the term as prophetic declaration. It is also sometimes translated as a warrant.

Yodun

Is a measure of distance equal to about sixteen miles or four *gav.* I have used the loose term league in my translation.

Bibliography

Basu, Soma. "A Critical Note on the Bhadrakalpavadana: A Store of Buddhist Studies in Verse." *International Journal of Buddhist Studies,* 1 4.4 (2003).

Berkwitz, Stephen C. *A History of the Buddha's Relic Shrine: A Translation of the Sinhala Thūpavaṃsa.* New York and London: Oxford University Press, 2006.

Carus, Paul. *Buddha, The Gospel.* Chicago: Open Court Publishing Company, 1894.

Chance, Jane. *Woman as Hero in Old English Literature.* Syracuse, NY: Syracuse University Press, 1986.

Cutler, Sally Mellick. *A Critical Edition with Translations of Selected Portions of the Pali Apadāna* 2. (*Yasodharāpadāna*). Unpublished dissertation for Oxford University, 1997.

Davy, John. *An Account of the Interior of Ceylon and of its Inhabitants with Travels in that Island.* London: 1821. Reprinted Colombo: Tisara Prakashakayo Press, 1983.

Gamlath, Sucharita, and Wickramasinghe, E. W., eds. *Yasodharāvata.* Colombo: Godage, 1995.

Lilley, M. E., ed. *The Apadāna of the Khuddaka Nikāya.* London: Pali Text Society, 1925.

Lopez, Donald, ed. *Buddhism in Practice.* Princeton: Princeton University Press, 1985.

Mayurapada Thēra. *Pūjāvaliya.* Colombo: Gunasena and Sons, 1986.

Malalasekere, G. P. *Dictionary of Pali Proper Names.* London: Pali Text Society, 1958.

Nabokov, Isabel. *Religion Against the Self: An Ethnography of Tamil Rituals.* Berkeley: University of California Press. 2000.

Pannaloka, Meegoda Thēra, ed. *Yasodharāpadāna*, Colombo: Sadeepa, 2000.

Paranavitana, S. *Sigiri Graffiti.* London: Oxford University Press, 1956.

Polvatte Buddhadatta Thēra, ed. *Yasodharāpadāna Gātā.* Colombo: Sihalavatta Prakāshaya, 1930.

Sala, J. M., ed. *Yasodhara Sinduva saha Satara Iriyavve Sivpada.* Colombo: New Lanka Press, 1949.

Somadasa, K. D., ed. *The Catalogue of the Hugh Neville Collection of Sinhala Manuscripts in the British Library*, vol. 3. London: Pali Text Society, 1990.

Strong, John. S. "A Family Quest: The Buddha, Yasodharā and Rāhula in the *Mūlasarvastivāda Vinaya.*" *Sacred Biography in the Buddhist Traditions of South and South East Asia,* ed. Juliane Schobar. Honolulu: University of Hawaii Press, 1997.

Swearer, Donald. "Bimbā's Lament." *Buddhism in Practice,* ed. Donald Lopez. Princeton: Princeton University Press, 1985.

Tattleman J. "The Trials of Yasodharā and the Birth of Rāhula: A Synopsis of the *Badrakalpa avadāna* II–IX." *Buddhist Studies Review*, 15.1 (1998).

———. "The Trials of Yasodharā: A Translation of the *Badrakalpa avadāna* II & III." *Buddhist Literature*, 1. (1998).

———. *The Truth of Yasodharā, A Critical Edition.* Annotated Translation and Study of the *Badrakalpa avadāna.* Doctoral thesis submitted to Wolfson College, Oxford University, 1996.

Wilce, J. M. "Genres of Memory and the Memory of Genres: 'Forgetting' Lament in Bangladesh." *Comparative Studies in Society and History*, 44 (2002) 159–185.

———. *Eloquence in Trouble: The Poetics and Politics of Complaint in Rural Bangladesh.* New York: Oxford University Press, 1998.

———. "Magical Laments and Anthropological Reflections: The Production and Circulation of Anthropological Text as Ritual Activity." *Current Anthropology*, 47 (2006).

———. "Traditional Laments and Post Modern Regrets: The Circulation of Discourse in a Metacultural Context." *Journal of Linguistic Anthropology*, 15 (2005) 60–71.